DEPARTMENTS THAT WORK

DEPARTMENTS THAT WORK

Building and Sustaining Cultures of Excellence in Academic Programs

Jon F. Wergin
Virginia Commonwealth University

Foreword by Estela Mara Bensimon

Anker Publishing Company, Inc.
BOLTON, MASSACHUSETTS

DEPARTMENTS THAT WORK

Building and Sustaining Cultures of Excellence in Academic Programs

ISBN 1-882982-57-6

Composition by Nicolazzo Productions
Cover design by Red Brick Design

Anker Publishing Company, Inc.
176 Ballville Road
P. O. Box 249
Bolton, MA 01740-0249 USA

www.ankerpub.com

DEDICATION

To my parents, Ed and Rae Wergin, whom I have been blessed to have in my life for more than 50 years.

CONTENTS

ABOUT THE AUTHOR

Jon F. Wergin is professor of educational studies at Virginia
Commonwealth University (VCU) and a senior scholar with the
American Association for Higher Education.

He received his PhD in educational psychology in 1973 from the
University of Nebraska, Lincoln, and has been at VCU ever since, serv-
ing in both administrative and faculty roles. In 1992 he took a leave
from VCU to be the founding director of the American Association for
Higher Education's (AAHE) Forum on Faculty Roles and Rewards and
has continued an active association with AAHE since then, focusing his
scholarship on evaluation and change in academic departments. His
monograph, *The Collaborative Department* (1994), was the first published by AAHE under the auspices of the Forum.

At VCU, Wergin teaches courses in adult and higher education and
coordinates the Preparing Future Faculty for the Professions program
(funded by FIPSE) through the graduate school. He has won school-wide
awards for both teaching (1996) and scholarship (1998). His other books
and monographs include *Educating Professionals* (1993, with Lynn
Curry), which won the Best Scholarly Publication award from Division I
of the American Educational Research Association; *Analyzing Faculty
Workload* (1994); *Analyzing and Evaluating Educational Research* (1996
and 2001, with Jim McMillan); and *Departmental Assessment: How Some
Campuses are Effectively Evaluating the Collective Work of Faculty*
(2000, with J. N. Swingen), which reports the results of a national survey
of departmental assessment practices for The Pew Charitable Trusts. He
has also published numerous journal articles on such topics as professional education, assessment, and the restructuring of faculty work. In
2001-2002 he directed another project funded by the Pew Charitable
Trusts, integrating efforts to assess student learning by the eight regional
accrediting associations.

Wergin is past divisional vice president of the American
Educational Research Association (Division I, Education in the

Professions), and has served as chief evaluator of two national centers for research in higher education. He is a distinguished visiting professor at Antioch University's doctoral program in leadership and organizational change and is a member of the National Academy for Higher Education Leadership. He has consulted with dozens of national associations, accrediting bodies, and colleges and universities on issues related to evaluation and change in higher education.

He lives in Richmond with his wife, Paula Horvatich, their two teenage children, and a 1940 Wurlizer jukebox.

FOREWORD

I was asked to read Jon Wergin's book while I was on sabbatical in Mexico. I took the manuscript with me to read during a four-hour bus ride from Mexico City to Morelia, a town in the northern part of Mexico. At the time, the prospect of reading and thinking about department chairs did not seem a very appealing way of passing the time. Much to my surprise and delight, *Departments That Work: Building and Sustaining Cultures of Excellence in Academic Programs,* is a page-turner—truly. This is not another book about strong, bold, and charismatic leadership. And that is a good thing. While those are admittedly fine traits, books that dwell on lofty issues of character too often fail to provide insight into how well-intentioned, nonsuperhero individuals can catalyze lasting transformation.

Departments That Work is active and positive. Department chairs make decisions about the nuts and bolts of undergraduate and graduate education—course scheduling, course offerings, program reviews, hiring and firing of adjunct faculty, evaluation of faculty performance, student complaints, etc. These responsibilities may be perceived as tasks that must be executed, however unpleasant they may be. Or they can be approached as opportunities to exercise leadership in the quest for excellence. For example, a department chair can treat post-tenure review as one more externally imposed rule and find ways of complying that will not disturb or disrupt the status quo. Or a department chair can decide to seize on the policy, misguided as it may be, as an opportunity to address larger issues about teaching and scholarship. Chairs who think in terms of compliance or doing what is expected often resort to dampening strategies of leadership. In contrast, Wergin's book is about how to develop chairs into active and creative leaders who can make a difference in the quality of their departments, despite the limits in formal authority and power inherent in the position.

Wergin's views on the role of the department chair and leadership are a welcome alternative to normative depictions of the department chair as the selfless colleague volunteering, albeit without much enthusiasm, to take his or her turn at being chair. Passive and unimaginative leadership may keep the peace, but as the environment of higher education becomes more competitive, uncertain, and unpredictable, such leadership may very well be a liability. Excellence grows and thrives in dynamic settings, the product of group effort; simply keeping the peace can be exclusive, boring, and deadening.

Departments That Work is realistic and inspiring. Although Wergin has faith in the power of leaders to bring about change, his conception of leadership is not based on idealized images of boldness, courage, and charisma that have very little to do with the political realities of academic departments. In fact, he tells us that to try to turn an academic department into a team—as that term is commonly used—is a losing proposition. Academic departments do not function as teams in the same way that sports organizations—or even business organizations—do. In important ways, Wergin's book talks about leadership in a new voice. Rather than telling department chairs how to be transformational, accrue power, and manage their department's culture, Wergin focuses the role of the department chair on how to create and maintain academic quality—the work of many stakeholders, not just the chair's. In so doing, he draws from a diverse and eclectic knowledge base which provides the book with a very solid intellectual foundation.

Departments That Work is a learning experience. To a great extent, the reason this book sounds different from the leadership books that populate the shelves of airport bookstands is that it draws on theories of adult learning rather than on theories of leadership. This is a novel approach and one which allows us to conceive of leadership as more human and possible as opposed to extraordinary and mythic.

Wergin has it right when he says that "true academic quality stems from authentic engagement of faculty and students with the subject matter and with each other." But engagement is not an easy condition to bring about. First of all, it is time-consuming and requires the creation of opportunities for engagement. Department chairs are primarily academics, and they have not been prepared to assume responsibility for the creation of engaging contexts apart from their own classrooms and labs. Ironically, this ability to engage others in the quest of excellence is probably the most important aspect of a chair's role. The unique value of *Departments That Work* is that Wergin provides extensive discussion about what motivates faculty, leading that discussion naturally into the notion of engagement.

Some might be inclined to dismiss the recommendations made by Wergin as overly idealistic; e.g., to make critical reflection part of the reward system, to make time for critical conversation groups, but this is what makes for a vibrant workplace. Such activity is also what department chairs may know the least about orchestrating or enabling.

New expectations of institutions and faculty which arise from the continuing concern with accountability, the quality of teaching, measures of learning outcomes, and the like will create a demand for chairs who, in addition to being astute managers of resources, also possess the skills and know-how to foster departmental cultures that motivate and reward good teaching, promote innovation, are affirming of newcomers, and invite commitment. *Departments That Work* speaks for and to this new breed of department chairs and does so in a very eloquent, learned, and practical manner. The reader will not find in this book descriptions of the leadership skills of exceptional individuals nor emotionally stirring accounts of leadership feats. What the reader will find, and which is what made this book such a pleasure to read, is the voice of an academic who is close to the ground, well-researched on the subject of department cultures, and possessed of a compelling voice. Every department chair should own a copy of *Departments That Work: Building and Sustaining Cultures of Excellence in Academic Programs*.

Estela Mara Bensimon
University of Southern California

PREFACE

What contributes to excellence in academic departments? Most faculty and their chairs and deans have at least a tacit idea of what "excellence" means. Great variability exists in beliefs about how to build and sustain it, however. For some, departmental excellence consists of little more than the cumulative accomplishments of the individual faculty, and so the best way to build it is to nurture the individual. Frankly, those holding this view will have little use for this book. For others, however, excellence—or as I'll define it later, program quality—depends on the extent to which the department or program functions as a collective and engages in work that makes the best use of the multiple talents and interests of its members. In this book I argue that the most useful way to build and sustain a culture of excellence is to create a culture of critical reflection and continuous improvement.

I have to confess something straightaway. When I first conjured up possible titles for this book, they all contained the words "quality" or "continuous improvement" in them. It didn't take long to realize just how marked words these had become, however. And while quality and continuous improvement in academic departments and programs are in fact much of what this book is about, I didn't want to scare people off with worn-out jargon, detritus of yet another management fad imported to a mostly unwilling academy. And so, yes, this book is about quality and continuous improvement, but I hope its ideas are presented in a way that is true to how higher education in general, and academic departments in particular, really work.

How might a culture of critical reflection in academic programs be built and nurtured? Most important to critical reflection is how a program learns about itself—how faculty come to a shared understanding of their collective work and how their work as individuals contributes to the whole. These understandings depend on data, specifically data that lead to useful value judgments. The problem is that while institutions may collect a great deal of information about program effectiveness, little of it may be useful within the department itself. In late 1998, I undertook a national study of departmental evaluation practices for the Pew Charitable Trusts. In this study, data concerning methods of departmental evaluation were collected from 130 institutions representing all Carnegie categories, from community colleges to research universities. While my colleague, Judi Swingen, and I found plenty of evaluation going on in these institutions, through such activities as program review, student outcomes assessment, and specialized accreditation, these methods often suffered from several debilitating problems.

First, most departments and most faculty did not see the relevance of such practices to their own work. In some cases, the faculty were so busy with their own agendas, and with the need to provide data for others to use, that the idea of using evaluation for formative purposes was lost. Further, faculty often viewed institutional measures of quality as off the mark, as not congruent with what their own definitions of quality might be. And finally, even institutions with effective, workable systems of program review showed huge variations across departments and schools. Consequently, most program review and outcomes assessment exercises have had only marginal impact on departmental practices. The institutional exceptions to this pattern were instructive, as they have a common theme: All were successful because faculty and departments had a strong influence on the purposes, processes, and methods of evaluation, and on the evaluation questions asked. Sometimes campus policies seemed to make little difference; what did matter was effective unit leadership, at both the school and departmental levels.

How academic programs might go about making evaluation more useful, and thus making critical reflection more likely, is the central purpose of this book. In brief, I argue that the only way to make quality assurance truly sustainable is to shift the emphasis from outside-in (that is, responding to state or institutionally-mandated assessment and evaluation) to inside-out approaches, designed and implemented by unit faculty themselves. I've organized the chapters as follows.

ORGANIZATION OF THE BOOK

In Chapter 1, I describe how "quality" in higher education has come to mean so many different things: how it has become confused with such concepts as effectiveness, productivity, and marketability; and how the faculty have largely surrendered their responsibility for ensuring academic quality to the likes of ratings published by news magazines. I suggest a new definition of quality, one that focuses on the engagement of the department with its constituencies.

In Chapter 2, in an attempt to untangle the apparent paradox of how highly reflective and analytic people can so often behave in unreflective ways, I review what we know about faculty motivation. I examine both intrinsic and extrinsic motivators of faculty work, the concept of organizational motivation, and the factors influencing identification with the institution and motivation to contribute to it.

In Chapter 3, I describe current practices in evaluation of academic departments, the building blocks of most colleges and universities. Here I summarize 130 institutions' experiences with program review, student outcomes assessment, and specialized accreditation, and isolate common problems with each of these. Based upon best practices identified in these institutions, I present three critical factors characterizing effective evaluation of academic units: organizational and cultural setting, evaluation policies and practices, and evaluation standards and criteria.

In Chapter 4, I examine the organizational and cultural setting in more detail. What does it take to create a culture of engagement? How might academic leaders nurture an atmosphere of critical inquiry? Develop a shared understanding of faculty work? Generate a sense of collective responsibility? Demonstrate a respect for difference? Develop a shared understanding of how the department adds value to the institution?

Chapter 5 takes up a topic not often addressed in books about academic programs: how academic values should be defined and negotiated. With multiple constituencies, academic departments must face the reality that quality is in the eye of the beholder: that stakeholders with different interests, or stakes, in the what the department does, will necessarily evaluate its work using different standards of value. This chapter describes how multiple and often conflicting values can be negotiated.

In Chapter 6, I suggest ways of asking the right questions and collecting the right data. How do faculty discover what is really important to know? What sort of information is useful to address questions of faculty productivity, efficiency, curricular and pedagogical quality, student productivity, and learning outcomes? Scholarly achievement? Adequacy of resources? Contribution to institutional mission and priorities? I also address issues of validity and reliability, and focus in particular on how to evaluate the quality of evidence used to make the department's case.

In Chapter 7, I take on a topic that is most often neglected in discussions of quality, and that is the issue of determining standards and making meaning of evaluation data. Too often it is assumed that standards will emerge naturally, with broad consensus, when in fact standard-setting is a highly political process. I discuss various sources of quality standards and their respective strengths and limitations, and how meaning-making is not a process that can be left to chance.

Finally, in Chapter 8, I summarize material from the previous chapters and offer some specific recommendations for academic leaders and departmental faculty. What can each group do to initiate critical reflection in their units and to keep it going?

An appendix, Departments That Work: What They Do, succinctly summarizes the constructs presented in each chapter.

CONCLUSION

I should also acknowledge my own biases in writing this book. While I have held a number of administrative positions during my career in the academy, my first and true loyalty is with the faculty. I care a great deal about the quality of faculty life, and I want to see it thrive. I will have some rather harsh things to say from time to time about faculty as a group, but I do so not to engage in the popular sport of faculty bashing, but rather to suggest that we simply must be more reflective about the work we do, both individually and collectively. This is not only in our constituencies' interest, but in our own as well. I can think of no better way for a Machiavellian administrator to disempower the faculty than to encourage a faculty culture that is dominated by fragmentation, specialization, and struggle for competitive advantage. A more conscious and sustained attention to departmental and program quality by the faculty not only demonstrates public accountability but also strengthens their individual academic freedom and autonomy. My hope is that by the end of this book, the reader will no longer see the irony in that statement.

Jon Wergin
Richmond, Virginia
April 2002

THE CONCEPT OF ACADEMIC QUALITY

The real voyage of discovery consists not in seeking new landscapes, but in having new eyes.

—Marcel Proust

INTRODUCTION

"Quality" is one of those terms which is easy to use but hard to define. It's been bandied about in all sorts of ways, particularly in the 1980s and 1990s when "total quality management" (or, for those in higher education who recoil at the term *management*, "continuous quality improvement") was all the rage. Quality is a concept that makes many academicians uncomfortable; for us, quality is one of those ineffable terms that's better left unexplained. We seem to agree with Robert Pirsig, who in his classic *Zen and the Art of Motorcycle Maintenance* said this: "Quality... You know what it is, yet you don't know what it is" (1974, p. 225). Most academics take what Garvin (1988) has called a transcendent view of quality, namely that because we are the experts, we know it when we see it—just don't expect us to tell you why we know it or how we know it. Society's interests are best served by advancing our own. The transcendent view

of quality might be easy for others to dismiss as haughty and self-serv-
ing, but there is actually substantial evidence for its validity. Years ago
Polyani (1967) wrote of "tacit knowledge," that form of knowing which
cannot be put into words. We all have had this experience: We sense
that we are onto something in our research; we can feel that students
are getting the *it* of what we are trying to teach them; or we suspect that
something is amiss with a loved one, even though we have no clear or
tangible evidence to back it up. Having a well-honed tacit knowledge of
the field is, in fact, one of the qualities which characterizes the true professional. When it comes to teaching and learning, therefore, we are the
best judges of what quality is, whether we're able to give voice to it or
not. Or so we would like to think.

Not only are faculty views of quality transcendent, they are also
largely silent. A survey reported by Massy (2001, personal communication) disclosed that more than half of all faculty respondents indicated
that they rarely—if ever—have discussions about quality; rather, they
view quality as a matter for individual faculty members to handle, mostly by keeping up with their disciplines, and it needs to be discussed only
when there's evidence of a problem.

FORCES FOR PUBLIC ACCOUNTABILITY

But transcendent and tacit views of quality no longer have much favor
with the public at large. There are many reasons for this but most stem
from what Robert Zemsky (1993) has termed the "loss of sanctuary."
That is, higher education is no longer immune from having to demonstrate public accountability and assure its usefulness to society. A college degree is no longer a ticket to economic success in most disciplines; it is no longer a sufficient condition for social prestige. It is, however, a necessary condition, and increasingly so. Students and their parents have become vociferous in their demands that higher education
deliver on its promises, especially given the record increases in tuition
costs during the 1990s and into the 21st century. Students are looking
for a competitive advantage, with marketable skills, not just the college
experience, and a competitive advantage is difficult to obtain when

college is for the many and not just the few.

And so the comfortable, even complacent attitude that many academics have about quality simply doesn't work anymore. "Trust us, we know best" isn't good enough, and the dangers of clinging to this mantra are serious. Consider Figure 1.1.

FIGURE 1.1
PUBLIC ACCOUNTABILITY IN HIGHER EDUCATION

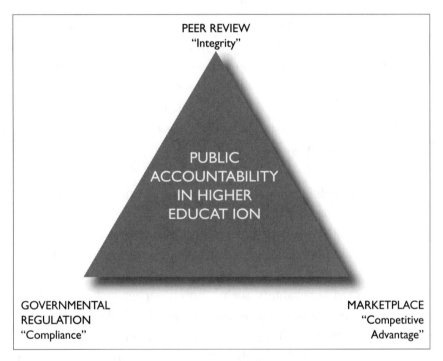

Higher education maintains its public accountability and assures its usefulness to society in three ways (Wergin, 1998):

1) Governmental regulation. This includes not only federal and state government, but also state coordinating and governing boards. This corner of the triangle exists to ensure that higher education institutions are fiscally and socially responsible, that they meet appropriate safety and health standards, and that they offer educational programs that aren't unnecessarily duplicative. The goal of regulation is *compliance*.

2) The marketplace. Particularly with the advent of technology and distance learning, the competition for students among educational providers is increasing. Institutions that fail to adjust to a changing market put their own health and survival at risk. The goal of the marketplace corner of the triangle is *competitive advantage*.

3) Peer review. I put peer review at the top of the triangle for a reason: Of the three forms of public accountability, this is the only one that focuses on the quality and integrity of the work itself, and it is the only one over which the institution and its faculty have any direct control. The collective faculty have traditionally been the ones responsible for maintaining program quality, and no one wants to leave that function to the government or the marketplace.

Here's a troubling paradox: Peer review, the form of public accountability in which the institution has—or should have—the greatest vested interest, is also usually the weakest. It's the area in which faculty, by retreating to notions of transcendent quality, have failed to develop ways in which that quality might be documented publicly. As I'll demonstrate in later chapters, such methods of peer review as accreditation and academic program review are viewed as little more than rituals in most institutions: They are seen as bureaucratic hurdles to clear, as necessary evils to put up with so that the real work of the academy can get done. According to William Massy (2001), the chief culprit isn't that faculty aren't interested in quality; it's that other priorities demand their attention:

> *[Faculty] are not—or at least in an organized way—carefully thinking through what we're trying to accomplish: writing it down, debating it, talking about it, thinking about measures we can use after the fact to determine how well we're doing, and then working on better designs for the teaching*

and learning process... [These activities] are intellectually interesting and challenging, but schools don't reward professors for doing them. Research gets rewarded, and faculty put their efforts where the rewards are. (p. 46)

This is a shame, because quality assurance from within, documented publicly, is potentially the most powerful way for higher education to maintain a core set of values that has served us well: Those values include autonomy, self-governance, and the pursuit of knowledge in a way that is unfettered by questions of efficiency or popularity.

We ignore our responsibilities for maintaining quality at our peril. No one in the academy wants the quality triangle to collapse into a straight line, with the government on one end and the marketplace on the other, but that's exactly what will happen if faculty decide they can't be bothered. Other sources of information on quality, like the now-popular (and to some in the academy, infamous) ratings published annually by *U.S. News & World Report*, will fill the breach.

WHAT QUALITY IS NOT

So what does "quality" mean, then? Is there a way to make the tacit observable, even measurable? Getting to the answer requires, first, a discussion of what quality is not.

Marketability

As I've implied already, quality is not the same as marketability. Quality is not doing whatever it takes to make our customers happy. True story: The music school of a large university in a major city was under fire for low enrollment and so decided to offer an undergraduate course in popular music appreciation as an elective to fill the humanities requirement. The course was taught by a local disk jockey in a large lecture hall to hundreds of eager students. Did the marketability of this course enhance academic quality? Most of us would sound a resounding "No." As Braskamp (1997) has observed, there's a difference between being respon*sive* and respon*sible*. Too much of the former threatens the latter. As the sociologist Everett Hughes once observed about the accountability of physicians: "A doctor who is too responsive to his patients is called a quack." Being responsible means working for the common good, which includes both addressing the expressed needs and priorities of those we serve *and* upholding the principles of academic freedom, "the free search for truth and its free exposition" (AAUP, 1995).

Productivity

Quality is also not the same as productivity, defined by economists as results per unit of input (usually money). More production—more students, more publications, more anything—is not necessarily better. In the above example the productivity of the music department's credit hour generation increased several times over. While one could argue that this allowed the department to turn its attention to more pressing matters and thus improve quality in other areas, the connection is indirect at best. Furthermore, a focus on productivity can lead to an obsession with counting and a neglect of the quality of the product being counted. The faculty member with the department's fattest curriculum vitae may not be doing the highest quality work; the faculty member teaching the most students may not be encouraging the highest quality learning.

Efficiency

Third, quality is not the same as efficiency. Efficiency is the cousin of productivity, with the cost variable thrown in. To be efficient is to achieve optimal productivity at minimal cost. Whether one is doing the right thing efficiently is another matter. Greater efficiency doesn't always translate to greater value, as the automobile industry learned years ago with the breakdown of quality along its assembly lines. A focus on the efficiency of teaching, which has led to the steadily increasing proportion of courses taught by low-priced teaching assistants and adjuncts, is in fact a major reason why our publics are so unhappy with us today. Further, the recent explosion of interest in distance learning as a tool for greater learning efficiency has led many to wonder whether we are doing ourselves or our students any favors. Still, becoming more efficient is a worthwhile goal if the right questions are asked (Ferren & Slavings, 2000), such as, "What would be the financial trade-offs of investing in programs designed to reduce the rate of freshman attrition?" Or, "What would be the fiscal consequences of increasing student success in 'killer courses'?"

Effectiveness

Fourth and finally, quality is not the same as effectiveness. Effectiveness is the extent to which an action accomplishes a desired purpose and produces the intended result. The problem is that not all purposes are quality purposes, and even if they were, not all actions are justified on their behalf. Amputating a finger is surely an effective cure for a pesky hangnail, but hardly the most desirable action one could take. Giving tests that measure recall of the material is surely an effective strategy for encouraging students to read the textbook, but hardly a useful strategy for encouraging deep learning and love of the subject. The point is that a blind adherence to doing what is effective may limit the extent to which we consider other, better, options.

CHARACTERISTICS OF A QUALITY DEPARTMENT

At this point the reader may be tempted to think, "Well, if quality isn't the same as any of these four characteristics, then maybe it's all of them combined." Consider for a moment an academic program that is marketable, productive, efficient, and effective. Is it a "quality" program? What's missing, if anything? Numerous considerations, including attention to the following factors, to name but a few:

- Faculty qualifications
- Social needs
- Growth of students and faculty
- Program cohesiveness
- Contribution to institutional mission

This is just a preliminary list; other items could be added. It would appear that quality must also address issues of academic integrity and the extent to which the program adds value to the larger organizational unit.

The problem with defining "quality," therefore, might not be that it is ineffable or inscrutable, only that it is complex and multidimensional. I have facilitated workshops in which I ask department chairs a straightforward question: "What are the characteristics of a quality department?" Collective responses from two groups of chairs are shown in Figure 1.2.

FIGURE 1.2
CHARACTERISTICS OF A QUALITY DEPARTMENT

Response from Group 1: about 60 chairs attending a national workshop

- Shared mission and vision
- External recognition
- High academic standards
- Excellence in teaching
- Active scholarship
- Collaboration and self-reflection
- Innovation; flexibility to change
- Collegiality
- Effective communication
- Balance in focus on students, community, institution, faculty
- A "quality" chair
- Successful students
- Adequate facilities and strong support staff
- Respect for diversity of opinion; "creative tension"

Response from Group 2: about 50 chairs, administrators, and faculty leaders from a consortium of colleges in the Northeast

- Focused mission
- Commitment to teaching and student learning
- Faculty academic development

- Resources for accomplishment of goals
- Harmonious, diverse, and well balanced community
- Best possible students and faculty consistent with institutional mission
- Successful students as graduates
- Active research by students and faculty
- Up to date and dynamic curriculum and pedagogy
- A program which benefits the community as well as students
- Open expression of ideas
- Strong ties with alumni and industry
- Continuous evaluation of programs and use of assessment data
- Support workers valued and acknowledged
- Department members committed to goals and values of college, global perspectives
- Effective, visionary leadership from faculty and chair

These are remarkably similar lists. What's striking about them both is the extent to which quality is characterized by what actually happens in the department: a shared purpose, strong leadership, interaction among faculty and students, flexibility to change, and a sense of energy and commitment. One might call this an engagement theme. Other themes, such as adequacy of resources, are present but less pronounced. It's instructive to contrast the items on these lists with how "academic quality" is traditionally defined and measured in the research literature. Haworth and Conrad (1997) have categorized studies of academic quality into four perspectives: 1) the faculty view, 2) the resources view, 3) the student quality and effort view, and 4) the curriculum requirements view. Sample commonly-used criteria from each perspective are shown below:

Four Perspectives of Academic Quality
The faculty view: criteria
- Educational training and qualifications

- Scholarly and research productivity
- Research funding
- Awards, honors, and prizes

The resources view: criteria

- Critical mass of faculty and students
- Financial resources
- Physical facilities

The student quality and effort view: criteria

- Educational qualifications and achievements
- Student involvement
- Quality of student effort

The curriculum requirements view: criteria

- Core and specialized course work
- Residency requirement
- Culminating experience

All four of these views are represented in the lists of quality characteristics generated by the department chairs and others in Figure 1.2, but none of them dominate the way the "engagement" theme does.

So why should faculty and chairs have such a different sense of quality from that held by researchers (and, for that matter, academic administrators)? The fact is, they don't. Sometimes in workshops that involve both chairs and central academic administration, I'll separate the two groups and ask each to respond to the following questions: 1) What are the criteria by which academic programs are evaluated? and 2) What are the criteria by which you *wish* academic programs were evaluated? The usual response to the first question by the chairs is, "We don't really know," and by the administrators, "Well, it depends" (a response often given with a little nervous laughter as they glance over at the faculty). The second question, on the other hand, usually produces similar responses which overlap considerably, usually to the surprise of the participants. When I then ask, "Well, if there's so much consensus about what constitutes academic quality, then why aren't programs evaluated that way?," the immediate reply is telling: "Because these other qualities are too difficult to measure." It's like the old joke about the drunk looking for his car keys under a streetlight because "that's where the light is." We evaluate academic programs according to such criteria as enrollment and student credit hours generated because that's where the data are.

TIME FOR A DIFFERENT VIEW OF ACADEMIC QUALITY

Maybe Persig was wrong in his observation about quality: We know what it is, and we can recognize it when we see it, but we think we can't measure it, and so we don't talk about it. But we complain when others do, like *U.S. News & World Report*.

I think that it's time for a different view altogether. By using my own and others' research I'll argue three points:

1) True academic quality stems from authentic engagement—of faculty and students with the subject matter and with each other, and of the department as a whole with its diverse and varied constituencies.

2) Quality is not a one-dimensional term. Quality means different things to different stakeholders, such as students, faculty, parents, board members, and the larger community. What constitutes a quality academic program therefore depends on a negotiation of interests and—conversely— quality programs result from negotiated values. Faculty and other members of the academic community have a critical stake in this negotiated definition, but they don't have the only stake.

3) Markers of quality, even the tacit, transcendent ones, are not only visible but measurable.

Before getting into these points in more detail, I need first to address the conditions under which faculty individually and departments as a whole will want to do quality work, whether or not they are pressured to do so.

REFERENCES

American Association of University Professors. (1940, 1995). *AAUP policy documents and reports.* Washington, DC: author.

Braskamp, L. A. (1997). On being responsive and responsible. *CHEA Chronicle No. 6.* Washington, DC: Council for Higher Education Accreditation.

Ferren, A. S., & Slavings, R. (2000). *Investing in quality: Tools for improving curricular efficiency.* Washington, DC: Association of American Colleges and Universities.

Garvin, D. A. (1988). *Managing quality: The strategic and competitive edge.* New York, NY: Free Press.

Haworth, J. G., & Conrad, C. F. (1997). *Emblems of quality in higher education: Developing and sustaining high-quality programs.* Needham Heights, MA: Allyn & Bacon.

Massy, W. F. (2001, July/August). Making quality work. *University Business, 4,* 44-50.

Pirsig, R. M. (1974). *Zen and the art of motorcycle maintenance: An inquiry into values.* New York, NY: Bantam.

Polyani, M. (1967). *The tacit dimension.* New York, NY: Doubleday.

Wergin, J. F. (1998). Assessment of programs and units. Presentation at the 1998 AAHE Assessment Conference. Reprinted in *Architecture for change: Information as foundation.* Washington, DC: AAHE.

Zemsky, R. (1993, May/June). On reversing the ratchet: Restructuring in colleges and universities. *Change, 25,* 56-62.

MOTIVATION FOR QUALITY WORK

If you seek it, obviously you don't see.

—Zen saying

INTRODUCTION

Reflect for a moment about what motivates you to do well in your own professional life. What is it that makes you want to get up and come to work in the morning? What keeps you going? What about your work do you find most rewarding? Think about these questions for a minute or two before reading further.

If you're like most academics, your list includes items like these: "Contributing to my discipline," "having an impact on students' lives," "the joy of learning." Some time ago I was asked to give a talk on the following topic: "It's Time to Develop Faculty Rewards That Act as Incentives!" The title seemed reasonable enough at the time; after all, one of the most common complaints among faculty members who have been encouraged to try new things is that the reward system is out of step. Faculty may become more engaged, more collaborative, more inventive with technology—but the institution will continue to reward teaching, service, and scholarship in the same old ways. Their concerns are usually not without foundation, and so I readily accepted the invitation. The more I thought about it, however, the more I realized that whenever we talk about faculty incentives and rewards we insist on using images that keep us stuck on dubious assumptions. The solution implicit in the phrase "develop faculty rewards that act as incentives" suggests that faculty life on campus resembles a giant Skinner box, in which faculty are the rats and administrators are the experimenters, devising ever more elaborate reinforcement schedules. This behaviorist approach to faculty work is often accompanied by other animal metaphors: leading faculty is like herding cats, the joke goes, or like shoveling frogs into a wheelbarrow.

But the university is not a microcosm of Walden Two and never has been, and the irony is that we should know better. Institutions can't simply manipulate rewards and expect faculty to fall into line. More than 40 years of research on the motivation of professionals, faculty included, has been remarkably consistent, showing that external incentives such as rank and salary are necessary but not sufficient conditions for inspiring quality faculty work (McKeachie, 1993). In fact, if we are to believe the research undertaken by Alfie Kohn (1993) and others, a focus on external incentives may in fact have results opposite to those intended. Junior faculty who do scholarship because that's what will get them promoted and tenured are less likely to value scholarship for its intrinsic sense of accomplishment. My guess is that the list you created two paragraphs ago contains few if any external incentives, but rather consists mostly of intrinsic motivators, reasons for engaging in work that have to do with the quality of the work itself (Froh, Menges, & Walker, 1993). In this chapter I'll review the research on faculty motivation and suggest what some of its implications are for institutions and their departments.

SOURCES OF FACULTY MOTIVATION

In their review of faculty motivation research, Baldwin and Krotseng (1985) suggest that a necessary precursor to quality work is faculty vitality. Vital professors "are enthusiastic, curious, and regenerative. [They] enjoy their work, reach out for new challenges, and are not afraid to risk failure" (p. 7). Over and over again, the research on faculty motivation has found that those of us who enjoy a vital faculty life are driven by a relatively small number of motives: autonomy, community, recognition, efficacy. Some studies come up with a longer list than this, some a shorter list. But nearly all mention these four.

Autonomy

This is the reason most often given when faculty are asked why they chose the academic life (Clark, 1987). Professional autonomy is the freedom to experiment, to follow one's own leads wherever they may go, and to do so without fear of the consequences. While autonomy is highly valued in nearly all professions, faculty members are likely the most purely individualistic of all professionals (Senge, 2000). Autonomy is what undergirds the principles of academic freedom, probably the most cherished academic value. It's important to note, however, that this freedom is not absolute, but relative. The 1940 AAUP *Statement of Principles of Academic Freedom and Tenure,* still in force today, says this: "Institutions of higher education are *conducted for the common good and not to further the interest either of the individual teacher or the institution as a whole.* The common good depends upon the free search for truth and its free exposition" (emphasis added). Thus, academic freedom does not mean that faculty members are free to do whatever they wish, and are answerable only to themselves. John Dewey defined freedom as the "power to grow," and this is what distinguishes autonomy from pure individualism. Unfortunately, some faculty don't see the difference. For them, autonomy refers to personal privilege, not a social obligation. But as I'll demonstrate shortly, autonomy *qua* pure individualism is not enough. The responsible expression of autonomy, the freedom to contribute to the common good, is what professionalizes faculty work.

Community

The second most common reason given for choosing faculty life is the desire to join a community of scholars, a notion that seems depressingly quaint to new faculty as they face an academic culture of isolation and competitive advantage. Some distressing research conducted over the years, first by Menges (1999) and most recently by Trower, Austin, and Sorcinelli (2001) shows clearly that the desire to be part of a scholarly community is one of the first to be thwarted as new faculty realize what they have to do to get ahead. As Bennett (1998) notes, autonomy and community come to be seen as being in conflict rather than complementary: "It is commonplace that over time the typical focus on inquiry becomes deeper and narrower... Separation rather than connection predominates, and an exaggerated sense of self-containment and even self-sufficiency follow... When we view the college or university through this model, it is no wonder that professors appear as autonomous individuals working in separate spheres" (p. 13). Research on academic departments conducted by William Massy and his colleagues at Stanford (1994) found a dominant departmental culture which Massy called "the hollowed collegium": cultures of emptiness, in which departmental colleagues maintained a surface civility but did so primarily as a veneer to keep from addressing issues which might lead to conflict, which in turn would take time away from individual faculty projects. As Bennett (1998) suggests, individualism and hollowed collegiality are only reinforced by an academy that celebrates the independent mind and considers those who collaborate as lacking real depth. The desire to belong, to feel part of a nurturing community, one in which the faculty member has an important role to play never goes away, however. Anything that eases the "pain of disconnection," as Parker Palmer (1998) calls it, is a powerful motivator, indeed. One of the most interesting findings from recent research in adult development is a phenomenon called "sex-role crossover" (Bee, 2000), in which the roles of early adulthood converge or even intersect in middle age: Men become less competitive and more nurturing, women become less nurturing and more autonomous. Consider for a moment the implications of this phenomenon: The source of the most energy for academic community in your department might be the aging male faculty!

Recognition

People everywhere want to feel valued, to know that others see their work as worthwhile. Faculty are no different. We need evidence that someone's paying attention. That's why so many salary disputes in higher education seem so symbolic: Money, even in minuscule increments, symbolizes recognition. Several years ago I was studying an experimental policy on faculty compensation at a comprehensive university in the Midwest. It had embarked on an departmental merit policy, in which half of all funds available for merit pay would be given as lump sums to entire departments, differentiated according to how meritorious their work as a unit had been the previous year. In most cases the differences in salary to be realized by individual faculty were tiny, only a few hundred dollars per year, yet judging by the heat of the debate, one would have thought that the stakes were enormous. But in a sense they were: People weren't fighting over the money; they were fighting over what the money represented. Other symbols of recognition, while simple, are surprisingly powerful: hearing unsolicited compliments from students or colleagues, getting quoted in a research article, fielding requests for assistance in an area of professional expertise. Recognition is public validation, and it's exceedingly powerful.

Efficacy

A term drawn primarily from the work of Albert Bandura (1977), efficacy is the sense of having had a tangible impact on our environment. We feel efficacious when we see students grasp a difficult concept, when we have added significantly to the knowledge base of the discipline, or when we have contributed positively to the quality of life in our communities. Efficacy is what gives our work meaning; it's a feeling that what we do matters. I used to work in an administrative position in my university, and many days I would go home from work wondering, "Now just what did I accomplish today?" It's not a good feeling. Contrast that to the times when you know that someone's life is different and better because of your role in it. That's efficacy. We couldn't survive emotionally without it.

These motivators are all interdependent, of course. Part of what makes an academic community strong is the professional autonomy of its members; and part of the power of recognition is the efficacy it communicates. It makes little sense, therefore, to design an academic environment conducive to quality faculty work unless all of these motivators are considered together. What follows is a list of motivational strategies which do this, in my opinion.

CONDITIONS PROMOTING QUALITY FACULTY WORK
Align Institutional Mission, Roles, and Rewards

Earlier I noted that extrinsic rewards alone won't promote quality work. That doesn't mean they're unimportant! They are, in fact, necessary, if not sufficient. When extrinsic rewards compete with intrinsic rewards, the former nearly always win, hands down. How often have you heard from tenure-track faculty that they'd prefer to spend more time working on their teaching but don't want to jeopardize their chances for promotion? Or even more disheartening, how many times have senior faculty told their junior colleagues not to waste time on their teaching until they're safely tenured?

The reward system is a powerful motivator of faculty behavior. Study after study during the past decade has demonstrated just how far out of whack faculty roles and rewards have become. A series of studies by Bob Diamond and his colleagues at Syracuse (1993) showed that faculty view teaching as relatively more important than research but see their institutions as having reversed priorities. A now-classic study by Jim Fairweather (1996) at Michigan State revealed that the more research faculty do, the more they earn, while the more teaching they do, the less they earn (a finding which is true, incidentally, of liberal arts colleges as well as research universities). Most recently, a survey by the Associated New American Colleges (McMillin & Berberet, 2002), a consortium of private comprehensive universities, showed that while faculty members in these institutions felt an alignment between their work and institutional mission, they perceived a misalignment between their work and institutional rewards. An interesting sidelight of this last study is that while about 70% of faculty felt they were in step with institutional mission, only 30% felt their colleagues were! (A cynical interpretation of this might be that most faculty feel they are the frogs who stay in the wheelbarrow; their colleagues are the ones who jump out.) Without alignment, faculty attachment to their institutions will be weak and more intrinsic motivation strategies will seem disingenuous, at best.

Alignment of roles and rewards is not the exclusive responsibility of academic administration, by the way. Promotion and tenure committees at most institutions are made up solely of senior faculty members. They are the ones who interpret policy, who decide whether or not a candidate meets the standards set forth in the policy documents. While it's true that their recommendations may be overturned by deans or provosts, such reversals are uncommon. Faculty who complain—with justification—about the mixed messages from their academic administration need also to scrutinize value choices that their own colleagues are making.

Engage Faculty Meaningfully

Faculty like work that is not only vibrant and intellectually interesting (that is, after all, why we're in this business), but work that takes us somewhere. I can't imagine any activity less motivating than one that everyone knows is purely ritualistic: the task force report that goes nowhere, the self-study that no one reads, the discussion of policies that are already a fait accompli. In the following chapter I'll describe in some detail our study of departmental review practices (Wergin & Swingen, 2000), where we uncovered some of the key ingredients to healthy departmental functioning. One of these was what we called a "leadership of engagement," a style of decision-making that relies on an open dialogue about the options faced and the likely consequences of options chosen. I think that much of what passes for faculty apathy about shared governance can be traced to a perception that what faculty say won't really matter. We don't like feeling co-opted and thus inconsequential to the life of the campus. We are much more energized by problems in which both we and the community at large have a stake, where we are presented with real choices, where our voice is recognized, and where we can act with a sense of efficacy. I am also aware of the hypocrisy in some faculty cultures, in which faculty demand to be consulted on all matters of import but want no part of the responsibility for the consequences. "Engaging faculty meaningfully" means that engagement must include a sense of collective responsibility for decisions made and actions taken—that leadership must also encourage collective reflection of the sort that leads to organizational learning.

Identify and Uncover Disorienting Dilemmas

A leading thinker in adult learning theory, Jack Mezirow (cf., 1990), has suggested that adults engage in deep (that is, transformative) learning only when faced with what he calls a "disorienting dilemma," a situation in which our usual perspectives won't work or don't fit. Only then, suggests Mezirow, are we likely to be motivated to learn and change. For example, experimental findings which don't square with accepted theory motivate us to look at the problem differently; student complaints about the incoherence of their undergraduate major motivate us to reassess our curricular requirements. Or maybe they don't: Adult perspectives about what is real or true are notoriously difficult to change, and so negative student feedback may well be met with denial or displacement of blame. Thus, the dilemma can't be too disorienting, because then it will only lead to an escape response.

Flow theory. A powerful theory of motivation developed by Csikszentmihalyi (1990), one that is backed by an impressive array of empirical research, helps put all this in context. This theory, called "flow theory," holds that the strength of intrinsic motivation is directly proportional to the extent to which the activity promotes a state of flow: a feeling of such total immersion in the task at hand that the individual becomes unaware of anything else. Most of us (more than 80%, according to Csikszentmihalyi) have experienced flow in our work—when a class session is going particularly well, for example, or when we become thoroughly engrossed in analyzing experimental data. The principal characteristic of flow is the perception of perfect congruence: that what we're doing is just challenging enough to give us a sense of accomplishment and growth. At these times we're at the top of our game, and that feeling alone is enough to sustain us. Insufficient challenge, on the other hand, leads to boredom and lack of energy; a challenge that is too far out of reach leads to anxiety and frustration. The trick, therefore, is to link challenge with support. If the goal is to encourage more faculty to use instructional technology, for example, then the appropriate strategy would be not only to show faculty how technology might enrich their teaching, but also to provide opportunities to experiment with such technology in a low-risk, high-support environment. Similarly, if the goal is to encourage greater faculty collaboration around departmental goals, the appropriate strategy would not be to have a series of meetings rewriting departmental mission statements and to exhort faculty to show how their work contributes to the mission, but rather to begin with the work faculty are doing, link it to collective expectations, and then help faculty see how they might contribute to the collective work more meaningfully.

In short, faculty resistance to change doesn't necessarily mean that they have no energy for change. Far from it.

Help Faculty Develop Niches

Back in the 1980s, several of my colleagues and I did a study of career satisfaction among senior faculty members in five diverse institutions, including a community college, a small private university, an Historically Black College/University (HBCU), a liberal arts college, and a research university. We wanted to know which factors most contributed to satisfaction among these faculty. What proved to be the most important factor separating high- and low-satisfaction groups across all institutions was what we called a sense of "niche," a perception that individual faculty had a place in their academic community which was theirs and no one else's. Two characteristics define a niche: 1) It's connected (that is, part of a larger organic whole), and 2) It's constantly evolving. What's the difference between a niche and a rut? Take a moment and mentally list the connotations you have for each term and you'll have the answer. A niche is warm, comfortable, three-dimensional, defined by a larger space; a rut is something you get stuck in. A niche promotes growth and change; a rut does not. Faculty can change their niches much like we decorate our houses or build an addition; in order for them to be comfortable, they have to be amenable to change. A faculty sense of niche connects with all four key motivators: It communicates autonomy, it requires a community context, it provides tacit recognition of worth, and, because faculty are the architects, it's a mark of efficacy.

Encourage Faculty Experimentation, Assessment, and Reflection

As I'll show in the next chapter, change is more likely to occur when faculty are encouraged to experiment and take risks. Instead of being held accountable for particular results, faculty are held accountable for conducting an assessment of their work, interpreting the results, and making informed judgments about what to do differently. Imagine the tone of an evaluation policy which focuses on faculty growth and development rather than exclusively on outcomes, such as articles published and grant dollars generated. How much healthier and more energizing that would be!

CONCLUSION: BUILD ORGANIZATIONAL MOTIVATION

At the beginning of this chapter, I derided the Walden Two approach to faculty motivation, the view that faculty behavior can be manipulated by adjusting reinforcement schedules. I hope I've shown that we're far better off thinking about motivation differently. The problem is not, How do we fix the reward system?; it's How do we create environments most conducive to productive faculty life? A useful way to think about this, and a useful way to end this chapter, is to consider Staw's (1983) notion of organizational motivation. Staw suggests that individuals are motivated to behave in ways befitting the interests of their organizations when two conditions are met optimally: when they identify with their institutions and when they see tangible evidence that they are contributing to their institutions in meaningful ways. Revisiting the list of four motivators (autonomy, community, recognition, efficacy), then, suggests the following.

- Faculty identify with their institutions when they understand that they are part of an academic community that cares about them and respects both their autonomy and the unique ways in which they contribute to the common good. They identify, in other words, when they feel a sense of niche.

- Faculty experience efficacy when they are recognized for the contributions they have made to the organization and perceive the effects these contributions have wrought. All this suggests that the way to enhance the collective motivation of faculty in academic departments is to create and nurture conditions which promote identification with the department and to ensure that faculty work is built upon the talents, interests, and expertise of its members. In the next few chapters, I'll explore ways to accomplish both goals.

NOTE

This chapter is a slightly expanded version of "Beyond Carrots and Sticks: What Really Motivates Faculty," published in *Liberal Education,* Winter 2001. Reprinted here by permission.

REFERENCES

American Association of University Professors. (1940, 1995). *AAUP policy documents and reports.* Washington, DC: author.

Baldwin, R. G., & Krotseng, M. V. (1985). *Incentives in the academy: Issues and options.* New Directions for Higher Education, No. 51. San Francisco, CA: Jossey-Bass.

Bandura, A. (1977). *Social learning theory.* Englewood Cliffs, NJ: Prentice-Hall.

Bee, H. L. (2000). *The journey of adulthood* (4th ed.). Upper Saddle River, NJ: Prentice-Hall.

Bennett, J. B. (1998). *Collegial professionalism : the academy, individualism, and the common good.* Phoenix, AZ: Oryx.

Clark, B. R. (1987). *The academic life: Small worlds, different worlds.* Princeton, NJ: Carnegie Foundation for the Advancement of Teaching.

Csikszentmihalyi, M. (1990). *Flow: The psychology of optimal experience.* New York, NY: Harper-Collins.

Diamond, R. M. (1993). Changing priorities and the faculty reward system. In R. M. Diamond & B. E. Adam (Eds.), *Recognizing faculty work: Reward systems for the year 2000.* New Directions for Higher Education, No. 81. San Francisco, CA: Jossey-Bass.

Fairweather, J. (1996). *Faculty work and the public trust: Restoring the value of teaching and public service in American academic life.* Boston, MA: Allyn & Bacon.

Froh, R. C., Menges, R. J., & Walker, C. J. (1993). Revitalizing faculty work through intrinsic rewards. In R. M. Diamond & B. E. Adam (Eds.), *Recognizing faculty work: Reward systems for the year 2000* (pp. 87-95). New Directions for Higher Education, No. 81. San Francisco, CA: Jossey-Bass.

Kohn, A. (1993). *Punished by rewards: The trouble with gold stars, incentive plans, A's, praise, and other bribes.* New York, NY: Houghton Mifflin.

Massy, W. F., Wilger, A. K., & Colbeck, C. (1994, July/August). Overcoming "hollowed" collegiality. *Change, 26* (4), 10-20.

McKeachie, W. J. (1993). *What we know about faculty motivation.* Presentation to first AAHE Forum on Faculty Roles and Rewards, San Antonio, TX (audiotape).

McMillin, L. A., & Berberet, J. (Eds.). (2002). *A new academic compact: Revisioning the relationship between faculty and their institutions.* Bolton, MA: Anker.

Menges R., & Associates. (1999). *Faculty in new jobs: A guide to settling in, becoming established, and building institutional support.* San Francisco, CA: Jossey-Bass.

Mezirow, J. (1990). How critical reflection triggers transformative learning. In J. Mezirow & Associates (Eds.), *Fostering critical reflection in adulthood: A guide to transformative and emancipatory learning.* San Francisco, CA: Jossey-Bass.

Palmer, P. J. (1998). *The courage to teach: Exploring the inner landscape of a teacher's life.* San Francisco, CA: Jossey-Bass.

Senge, P. M. (2000). The academy as learning community: Contradiction in terms or realizable future? In A. F. Lucas & Associates (Eds.), *Leading academic change: Essential roles for department chairs* (pp. 275-300). San Francisco, CA: Jossey-Bass.

Staw, B. M. (1983). Motivation research versus the art of faculty management. In J. L. Bess (Ed.), *College and university organization: Insights from the behavioral sciences.* New York, NY: NYU Press.

Trower, C., Austin, A., & Sorcinelli, M. (2001, May). Paradise lost: How the academy converts enthusiastic recruits into early-career doubters. *AAHE Bulletin, 53* (9), 3-6.

Wergin, J. F., & Swingen, J. N. (2000). *Departmental assessment: How some colleges are effectively evaluating the collective work of faculty.* Washington, DC: AAHE.

EVALUATING QUALITY IN
ACADEMIC PROGRAMS

From naive simplicity we arrive at

more profound simplicity.

—Albert Schweitzer

INTRODUCTION

See if this scenario describes what happens in your own department: Every five to seven years your unit comes up for a formal program review. It's an event that does not inspire much enthusiasm among the faculty. There's plenty of busywork as the self-study is prepared, and there's a lot of grumbling about wasted time and bureaucratic intrusion. Everyone's goal is to get through the process with a minimum of aggravation. When it's over, the final report disappears into the bowels of the administration and nothing much changes, but at least the faculty won't have to worry about it again for awhile. This whole pageant is repeated, with minor variations, for regional and specialized accreditation, student outcomes assessment, and various ad hoc strategic planning initiatives.

If all this seems distressingly familiar, you're not alone. There's more evaluation in higher education today than ever before, but it's had remarkably little impact, as several studies (National Center for Postsecondary Improvement, (NCPI) 1999; Peterson & Einarson, 2001) have shown. In the NCPI study, a survey of more than 1,000 chief academic officers revealed that while most institutions regularly collected data on college-readiness skills and students' academic intentions, far fewer (one-third or less) collected data on the students' experiences or what they learned. Even more disheartening, most respondents could not connect the collection of assessment data with decisions about academic programs or budget: Instead, the most commonly-cited reason for doing assessment was for accreditation purposes.

USUAL REASONS FOR NOT USING ASSESSMENT DATA

As Joseph Burke (1999) asks in what he calls "the Assessment Anomaly," "If everyone's doing it, why isn't more getting done?" There are two usual suspects often used as excuses for this sorry state of affairs: the complexity of measuring student learning outcomes, and the old stand-by, faculty resistance. I'll take up each of these in turn.

The Complexity of Measuring Student Outcomes

The argument for the former goes like this: The thrust of the assessment movement has been to shift the focus from inputs, such as resources and capacities, to outcomes, namely impacts on student learning. This is all well and good, but the problem is that we don't know how to measure student learning very well, certainly not in the aggregate, and so if the point of student outcomes assessment is to reveal what students as a group have gained from their college experience, and to do so in a way that would lead to some comparability across programs and institutions, the measurement challenges become horrendous. Besides, to continue the argument, real learning has certain ineffable qualities anyway, which defy any of our crude attempts at measurement.

Faculty Resistance

The argument for faculty resistance as a major barrier to useful assessment (or, for that matter, virtually any campus initiative), goes like this:

Faculty members treasure their autonomy, and are not about to give this up just because some administrator talks about the need to become more accountable. More than any other part of their work, their teaching is their own domain, and faculty feel as if they have proprietary rights to their courses. Student grades are sufficient evidence of learning; demanding any more evidence than that presents a potentially serious threat to academic freedom.

CENTRAL REASONS WHY PROGRAM ASSESSMENT IS NOT EFFECTIVE

Both of these barriers are real, and the arguments which underlie them have some merit (cf. Dill, Massy, Williams, & Cook, 1996). They are not the real culprits, however, in my view. The central reasons why program assessment has not been more effective are elsewhere.

A Compliance Mentality

The questions driving many program reviews, as well as other forms of program evaluation, are perceived as theirs, not ours. The review is on someone else's agenda: the higher administration, the governing board, the accrediting commission. Most faculty accept the necessity of program review, but don't necessarily see it as a process that will affect their own professional practice, at least not in a positive way. A second and related problem is that most quality reviews are one-shot affairs, not well integrated into the life of the institution. And furthermore, because the review is backward (on what has already happened) rather than forward (on what is possible), the opportunity for critical reflection—a chance to put our strong academic values of systematic inquiry and questioning of assumptions to use—is lost in the desire to get the thing done. Thus, the process often unfolds in a way that encourages participants to get through it with a minimum of aggravation. The self-study is given over to selected staff and a few faculty members who, if they are lucky, will be given some release time to conduct the study and write the report. The whole thing becomes tedious, time-consuming, and too often ultimately of little or no consequence. It becomes a ritual, a special event that isn't integrated with the work of the faculty. Massy captures the phenomenon this way: a "culture of compliance" becomes a "culture of *apparent* compliance" (2001, personal communication).

An Individualistic Faculty Culture

As I noted in Chapter 1, faculty culture in most departments and programs is individualistic and highly privatized. Evaluation devolves to the individual, not the unit. Faculty are rewarded on the basis of their contributions to their profession or discipline, not to their institutions. An anonymous pundit has gone so far as to say this: "Academic departments are clans of arrogant experts seeking to sustain individual privilege at the expense of institutional goals." An overstatement? Sure. But I'll bet that it isn't much of a stretch to identify departments like this at your own institution. Moreover, as Fairweather (1996) has pointed out, when units as a whole are evaluated, they are normally judged on the basis of the sum of the performances of individual faculty—scholarly productivity, for example—not by measures of the unit's contributions to a larger good. The emphasis continues to be on individual merit, not on collective worth to the mission of the institution. As a consequence, there's little faculty investment in activities that require collective action.

Consequential Validity

Messick (1994) suggests that besides the traditional forms of validity and reliability of evaluation measures, we need also to consider the effect of the measure on behavior. For example, suppose that the police department in your town were evaluated on the basis of arrest rate per policeman. Would the arrest rate go up or down? And what would this indicate about the quality of police work in the town? Or, to take an example from within the academy, suppose that teaching quality were judged solely on the basis of student ratings of instruction. Faculty would feel significant pressure to increase their student ratings and so would be tempted to do whatever was necessary to achieve this outcome. Faculty would end up chasing the measures, thus making them the surrogate goal. Research has shown that student ratings are at least somewhat manipulable (McMillan, Wergin, Forsyth, & Brown, 1986) and in ways that might have little to do with teaching quality. Worse, focusing on ratings could actually serve as a disincentive to doing quality work, if faculty feel that making changes in their courses would not be worth the almost-certain (albeit temporary) drop in student ratings that would follow. This phenomenon is known in the management literature as "goal displacement" (Blau & Scott, 1962). Examples of goal displacement are numerous in the academy. As long as institutions are funded on the basis of student credit hour generation they will have little incentive to help students pass, to reduce the number of courses repeated, or to reduce the number of courses required for graduation (Ferren & Slavings, 2000). In Chapter 1, I noted how the mentality of the marketplace has created a rush of institutions wanting to improve their tier status as defined by *U.S. News & World Report* rankings. The rankings have themselves become the goals, even if the criteria which define them have little to do with the true mission of the institutions. At the same time, if measures are not taken seriously and have no consequences at all, the motivation to collect valid data disappears. Ignoring the unintended consequences of using program and institutional measures has far-reaching—and mostly pernicious—effects.

THE PEW STUDY

With all this in mind, and with the generous support of The Pew Charitable Trusts, my associate, Judi Swingen, and I set out to assess the state of program assessment in the US. We reviewed the literature, called upon personal networks of informants, and sent a mass mailing to all campus provosts, inviting them to share examples of effective evaluation practice with us. We eventually studied 130 institutions across the Carnegie categories, from community colleges to research universities. From some we merely collected information on paper, for others we conducted telephone interviews with key campus participants, and for eight institutions we wrote extensive case studies based on two-day visits to their campuses. A full account of this research study may be found in our 2000 monograph, *Departmental Assessment: How Some*

Colleges Are Effectively Evaluating the Collective Work of Faculty
(Wergin & Swingen, 2000). A summary of this study follows, leavened
somewhat by a distance of two years.

In our view, effective evaluation informs judgments of quality which
then lead to improved departmental functioning. Using that standard,
we found the state of program evaluation in higher education to be dis-
mal, indeed. While there was plenty of evaluation going on, discontent
with its usefulness was widespread. Among several roots of campus
unhappiness, one was most striking: Most departments and most faculty
failed to see the relevance of program evaluation and assessment to the
work they did. Our earlier suspicions proved correct: Departmental
assessment was largely a ritualistic and time-consuming affair, mandated
from above, having few real consequences for the lives of the faculty.

ANALYZING EFFECTIVE UNIT EVALUATIONS

Despite this rather bleak portrayal, we found some notable exceptions
to the norm, places where unit evaluation informed judgments of worth
and improved departmental functioning, and so we studied them carefully to try and discern what made them stand out from the pack. We
found it most useful to cut the analysis in three ways: 1) to articulate the
necessary conditions for effective evaluation; 2) to determine which
institutional policies and practices served as the *best predictors of effectiveness;* and 3) to pinpoint the issues that remained *most problematic*,
even at the exemplary institutions.

Necessary Conditions: Organizational and Cultural settings

Certain institutional features seemed essential; while alone they did not
guarantee effective evaluation practice, they certainly seemed necessary. We found examples of campuses where evaluation went nowhere,
even with otherwise exemplary policies, and we traced the barriers to
the lack of effective leadership in either central academic administration, academic departments, or both. Campuses with successful practices concerned themselves first with building an institutional climate
supportive of quality improvement. For example, when the provost at a

private research university with a history of successful program review was asked how he would go about initiating evaluation in another institution, he said this: "First I'd take a measure of the institution and its vision for the future. Is there ambition for change? I would try to find ways of articulating a higher degree of aspiration; if there weren't a strong appetite for this, then program review would be doomed to failure."

Six elements of a quality institutional climate were suggested by the institutions we reviewed.

1) A leadership of engagement. The leaders are able to frame issues clearly, put clear choices before the faculty, and be open to negotiation about what will inform these decisions. Of all the elements of organizational climate, this one was the most important.

2) Engaged departments. Departments ask very basic questions about themselves—"What are we trying to do? Why are we trying to do it? Why are we doing it that way? How do we know it works?" In essence, these departments have created a climate for reflection, a notion I'll explore in detail in Chapter 7.

3) A culture of evidence (a term first used by Ralph Wolff at the Western Association of Colleges and Schools). The institutions shared a spirit of reflection and continuous improvement based on data, an almost matter-of-fact acceptance of the need for evidence as a tool for decision-making. We found that a culture of evidence bore little if any relationship to the amount of evidence collected on campus; the key lay in what the institution did with the information collected.

4) A culture of peer collaboration and peer review. Common criteria and standards for evaluation are based on a shared understanding by departmental faculty of one another's work. Successful departments had a truly collaborative culture: It wasn't necessarily that they all worked together, but rather that they had a clear sense of what their colleagues did, how the collection of individual work created a coherent whole, and how their own work contributed to that collective (for an interesting discussion about these two conceptions of collaboration, see Bensimon & O'Neill, 1998).

5) A respect for difference. Faculty roles are differentiated, leading to a shift in focus from work that is judged by standards external to the unit (merit) to the contribution of the faculty member to the mission of the unit (worth). This merit/worth distinction is key to understanding the difference between the rampant specialization that has plagued academic departments in the last half-century, and true role differentiation, which takes the departmental context into account. I'll explore this notion more fully in a later chapter.

6) Evaluation with consequence. Evaluation has a tangible, visible impact on resource allocation decisions. This principle seems so obvious as to be almost not worth mentioning, yet as I noted earlier, it's amazing how something so obvious is so often ignored. We discovered also that consequence has its limits: The process can't be so consequential that it turns into a high-stakes political exercise. When this happens, incentives for improvement are lost in the rush to look as good as possible.

In the next chapter, I examine these characteristics in more detail and suggest ways in which departments might enhance them.

Evaluation Policies and Practices

We have all had this experience: We finish a study, put it away for awhile, then go back to it and find new insights. Such was the case here. We had become so engrossed in the details of our study that we missed an unmistakable fact, there all along: Among the institutions meeting the necessary conditions described above, one single factor discriminated the institutions where evaluation was effective from those where it wasn't.

In short, what made evaluation effective in some places and not in others was the degree to which evaluation policies were *flexible* and *decentralized*. In these institutions, units were invited to define for themselves the critical evaluation questions, the key stakeholders and sources of evidence, and the most appropriate analysis and interpretation procedures.

The clearest example we found of this was a small private university which had been laboring with a traditional program review policy for years, one that mandated a comprehensive self-study for the department under scrutiny, completed according to criteria mandated by the institution, and followed up by a visit from an external review team and an extensive report filed away in central administration. No one at this institution was happy with the paltry return on investment of all this time and money, including the administration, and so they decided to try something different: a focused program review, in which departments up for evaluation would first submit a proposal identifying the key issues they faced as a department and a plan for studying these issues. As negotiated with the department's dean, this proposal would serve as the basis for the department's self study. The only institution-wide requirement was that departments include in their study an analysis of how they were contributing to the mission of the institution. After two years' experience with this experimental policy, the results were clear: Departments taking the focused approach made significant changes to their collective work, while those taking the traditional comprehensive approach did not. Some administrators at this institution remained skeptical, suggesting first that the differences could be due to nothing more than the Hawthorne effect (any positive change as a result of merely showing attention to the problem), then later that weak departments would use the focused approach as a way to avoid scrutiny of their problems. It turned out that just the opposite was true: the strong departments were those which opted for the focused approach, because they had a clearer sense of collective mission and saw in the new policy an opportunity to collect information that would help them become stronger.

There's a clear lesson from the above story. Institutions should focus less on accountability for achieving certain predetermined results and more on how well units conduct evaluations for themselves and use the data these evaluations generate. Rewards then accrue to units that can show how they have used the assessment to solve problems and resolve issues.

This notion is similar to academic audit procedures currently in widespread use in Western Europe and Hong Kong, and gaining popularity in this country among accreditation agencies: Rather than attempting to evaluate quality itself, the focus instead is on processes believed to produce quality: "[Academic audits] look deep into the heart of the academic enterprise. They test whether institutions and their faculties in fact honor their public responsibility to monitor academic standards and improve student learning" (Dill, Massy, Williams, & Cook, 1996, p. 35).

Evaluation Criteria and Standards

"Criteria" are the kinds of evidence collected as markers of quality; "standards" are the benchmarks against which the evidence is compared. We found many problems with the use of evidence, even in the most exemplary cases. It wasn't that institutions lacked information that might lead to judgments about departmental quality: Our database contained examples of more than 100 quality indicators, and these were distributed fairly evenly across input (faculty qualifications, FTEs), process (curriculum quality, demands on students), and output (faculty publications, student learning) criteria. The problem rather was that we found not a single case in which institutional procedures called for examining the quality of the evidence itself—not one! The underlying assumption seemed to be that the more information collected, the better, and that some kind of invisible hand would lead to true and valid conclusions.

Further, we found a widespread lack of clarity and agreement about what the standards should be. For example, what is the most appropriate standard for departmental research productivity: departmental goals negotiated earlier with the dean? last year's performance? the extent to which the scholarship fits within school priorities or the university's strategic plan? or how well the department stacks up against its peer departments in other institutions? As I pointed out in Chapter 1, standards considered important or credible by one stakeholder group may not be considered important at all by another; thus, departmental quality will always be in the eye of the beholder. Just as it's dangerous to ignore issues of data quality, it's also risky to assume that all involved have the same implicit standards.

In Chapters 5 and 6, I discuss the questions of criteria and standards in some detail and offer some ideas for making evidence more useful and decisions more sound.

IMPLICATIONS

The research reported in this chapter serves as the backbone for the remaining chapters in this book. The logic is as follows: If the 130 institutions we studied are at all representative of American higher education, then the most substantial barriers to quality have to do with how we think about evaluation. As long as we maintain an outside-in focus, in which evaluation and assessment occur only when mandated externally, and a compliance mentality, which encourages a rote, get-it-over-with approach to evaluation, we will never become truly reflective about the work we do, and we will never achieve an academic culture in which attention to quality is part of its fabric. In the remaining chapters, therefore, I take up the key issues raised by the Pew study and suggest how the academy in general, and academic departments in particular, might deal with them in a way that would lead to cultures of quality.

REFERENCES

Bensimon, E. M., & O'Neill, H. F., Jr. (1998). Collaborative effort to measure faculty work. *Liberal Education, 84* (4).

Blau, P. M., & Scott, W. R. (1962). *Formal organizations: A comparative approach.* San Francisco, CA: Chandler.

Burke, J. C. (1999, July/August). The assessment anomaly: If everyone's doing it why isn't more getting done? *Assessment Update, 11,* 4.

Dill, D. D., Massy, W. F., Williams, P. R., & Cook, C. M. (1996, September/October). Accreditation and academic quality assurance: Can we get there from here? *Change, 28* (5), 17-24.

Fairweather, J. (1996). *Faculty work and the public trust: Restoring the value of teaching and public service in American academic life.* Boston, MA: Allyn & Bacon.

Ferren, A. S., & Slavings, R. (2000). *Investing in quality: Tools for improving curricular efficiency.* Washington, DC: Association of American Colleges and Universities.

McMillan, J. H., Wergin, J. F., Forsyth, D. R., & Brown, J. C. (1986). Student ratings of instruction: A summary of literature. *Instructional Evaluation, 9* (1), 2-9.

Messick, S. (1994). *Validity of psychological assessment: Validation of inferences from persons' responses and performances as scientific inquiry into score meaning.* Research Report RR-94-45. Washington, DC: ERIC ED380496.

National Center for Postsecondary Improvement (1999, September/October). Revolution or evolution? Gauging the impact of institutional student-assessment strategies. *Change,* 53-56.

Peterson, M. W., & Einarson, M. K. (2001). What are colleges doing about student assessment? Does it make a difference? *Journal of Higher Education, 72,* 629-669.

Wergin, J. F., & Swingen, J. N. (2000). *Departmental assessment: How some colleges are effectively evaluating the collective work of faculty.* Washington, DC: AAHE.

CREATING THE ENGAGED DEPARTMENT

The most pathetic person in the world
is someone who has sight but no
vision.

—Helen Keller

INTRODUCTION

In Chapter 1, I suggested that true academic quality stems from the authentic engagement of the department with its constituencies; in Chapter 3, I noted how departmental engagement is one of the critical factors contributing to a quality institutional climate (Wergin & Swingen, 2000). Our study is only one of several to have uncovered the importance of engagement. Others include Bensimon and Neumann (1993), Massy, Wilger, and Colbeck (1994), Bennett (1998), Walvoord et al. (2000), and especially Haworth and Conrad (1997). One of the reasons why engagement has drawn so much attention in recent years is the sheer absence of it. The professoriate is rife with ironies; surely one of the most puzzling is why a community of people who are all committed to a life of engagement with learning could be so unengaged with each other, or with the department to which they belong. If indeed the academic profession is the most individualistic of all organizational cultures (Senge, 2000), why is this the case? Why is it that when you talk about departmental collaboration people treat it as an oxymoron? Why is it that, even though I wrote *The Collaborative Department* (Wergin, 1994) nearly ten years ago, I continue to be kidded by colleagues who say that it was the only book of pure fantasy ever published by the AAHE? How did we get this way? There are at least three reasons, one personal, two environmental.

WHY DEPARTMENTAL COLLABORATION IS SCARCE

Faculty Individualism

First, faculty members are by nature an introverted lot (Clark, 1987). We enjoy being by ourselves and left to our own devices. It isn't that we can't be social; it's just that we gain energy from ideas more than people. Moreover, the freedom and flexibility we enjoy attracts those who, in Bennett's words, are "already disposed to be insistent individualists" (1998, p. 19), and these dispositions are reinforced by graduate school norms:

> . . . to study carefully and critically the received past with an eye toward challenging and revising the tradition, to develop and defend one's own distinctive ways of interpreting the data and phenomena of the discipline, and 'to make a name for oneself.' Almost always, the major emphasis is disciplinary in character. Far less emphasis is placed on the ethos that supports the university as an intellectual and moral community committed to a common task. (p. 19)

Research Emphasis

Second, the end of the Second World War created a boom in research that was unprecedented and is still going on today. Its impetus was the report released by Vannevar Bush (United States Office of Scientific Research and Development, 1945) which suggested that the way for the US to retain the power and influence it had gained from the war was to invest heavily in basic research—especially in the sciences and engineering—and that the best setting for this research was the university. It wasn't long before millions of dollars were flowing into those institutions. Alpert (1986), a scientist himself, in a widely-cited essay has decried the lure of the federal grant as having shifted the central mission of the university and its faculty away from teaching to research. Faculty, like everyone else, follow the money, and for at least the last 50 years the big money has been in federal research grants.

Mission Creep

Third, due in part to the prestige accorded universities with major research agendas, academic institutions have been engaged in what has been called "mission creep"—the unending desire to improve the status of the institution by moving up the Carnegie ladder. Colleges want to be universities; master's universities want to be doctoral universities; doctoral universities want to be research universities; and research universities want to be in the Top Ten (or if they have more modest aspirations, in the Top 25 or the Top 50) of universities ranked by the National Research Council. The path to excellence is clear: Get the big-ticket federal grants that will let you hire adjuncts and teaching assistants who will take over the teaching of undergraduates, and leave the work of the university to those who can't do cutting-edge scholarship anymore.

The consequences are clear and unequivocal. In a recent study undertaken of a broad sample of faculty at a cross section of institutions (UCLA, 1997), respondents were asked to identify a valued colleague in their department and then to select from a list of descriptors those which characterized this person. The three most-selected descriptors were "dedicated," "ambitious," and "competitive," all selected by more than 80% of the respondents. "Team player," in contrast, was far down the list, selected by only 56%. Massy, Wilger, and Colbeck (1994), in an attempt to identify some of the characteristics of an effective department, interviewed 300 faculty members in 20 institutions and found the dominant feature of departmental cultures to be atomization and isolation. Most respondents had little stomach for engaging in the constructive contention they needed to fully engage the issues they faced in their work together. The result was what authors called "hollowed collegiality": a veneer of civility that masked a deep reluctance to collaborate, for fear of diverting time and energy away from their research priorities.

What emerges from all this research, and from most people's anecdotal experience as well, is the image of college faculty as isolated bands of academic entrepreneurs working from their own private agendas. One response to this might be simply to shrug it off: So what? The academic culture as we know it has built a higher education system that is the envy of the world. Why tamper with success? Why not just hire the best faculty you can (that is, faculty having the most prestigious scholarly pedigrees) and turn them loose? Thinking differently about the faculty collective—the faculty as a collective—strikes some as a bureaucratic if not downright socialistic idea, simply the latest in a long and lamentable string of half-baked management schemes all meant to fatten administrators' resumés and reduce faculty power and autonomy. In response to these arguments, none without merit, I'd like to make these six points:

> 1) Despite the prevailing myth to the contrary, faculty work is not especially portable. Only a fraction build a portfolio which allows them upward, or even lateral, movement across institutions. The work faculty do is contextual to the institution, whether they like it or not.

> 2) The same is true of departments. The work of a psychology department in College A is different from the work of another psychology department in College B, even if it has a similar size and mission. The collective work faculty do is contextual as well.

> 3) Faculty entrepreneurship in the absence of collective responsibility threatens curricular coherence. One of the most telling criticisms of the late 20th century was that American higher education has paid insufficient attention to its undergraduate mission (Association of American Colleges and Universities, 1985): that institutions (and their departments)

are so busy focusing on their research agendas and farming out their undergraduate courses to teaching assistants and adjuncts that the undergraduate curriculum lacks cohesion and any real semblance of quality control. What makes this especially galling to the critics is that undergraduates in these departments are often seen as cash cows who support the specialized graduate programs faculty treasure so highly. There is only one way for curricula to become more coherent, and that is for faculty to become less proprietary about their courses and talk with each other about what and how they teach.

4) As I noted in Chapter 2, the desire for community is one of the most powerful faculty motivators, and even if young faculty see their dreams of a community of scholars evaporate as they realize what they have to do to gain a competitive advantage, the desire for connection never goes away (Schuster, Wheeler, & Associates 1990): It simply becomes dormant. Several years ago, Jane Tomkins published a widely-read essay in which she wrote poignantly about the loneliness of academe, and her craving for belonging to a larger group bound by a common purpose (Tomkins, 1992). Providing a means for faculty members to realize their long-latent desire for community can be a powerful and positive force for change.

5) It's important not to confuse faculty autonomy with privatization. Autonomy is fundamental to academic freedom and cannot be abridged. Faculty need the freedom to pursue their work, unfettered by what is considered to be popular or marketable at the time. Faculty members earn their professional autonomy by engaging in work that benefits society. In a culture of privatization, however, faculty feel responsible only to themselves and what benefits their careers. I'll argue later that having faculty work defined within the parameters of the department, so that all contribute in ways which best

draw upon their individual interests, talents, and expertise (because not everyone should be expected to excel at everything), may result in more rather than fewer options. Sartre once wrote about the "tyranny of freedom"; contextualizing faculty work within the mission of the department can nullify this tyranny and make faculty work more personally liberating.

6) Finally, if none of the above reasons is persuasive enough, there's this: Faculty who work for a collective rather than a private good increase their political clout. It's hard to imagine a culture more disempowering of faculty, one that leaves them in a weaker position in the face of external threats, than the one we have. As long as faculty members are individual agents, responsible only to themselves, they will have little power as a group. Thus, shifting the focus from "my work to our work" (Rice, 1996), is not only good for the institution, it's also in the best interest of the faculty.

The challenge, therefore, is how to engage the department in ways that do not continue to support the current communities of convenience but instead help the department evolve a sense of collective responsibility (Wergin, 1994). What does an engaged department look like, and what can a department do to become more engaged? I'll take as a point of departure the work of Haworth and Conrad (1997), who propose that high-quality programs are characterized by five attributes: 1) "diverse and engaged participants, 2) participatory cultures, 3) interactive learning and teaching, 4) connected program requirements, and 5) adequate resources" (p. 28). Of these, the authors suggest, the first two are critical:

> In high-quality programs, faculty and administrators continually seek to attract and support faculty and students who infuse diverse perspectives into—and are engaged in—their own and others' teaching and learning... Program administrators, faculty, and students... develop and sustain cultures that emphasize a shared program direction, a community of learners, and a risk-taking environment. (p. 28)

Haworth and Conrad built their theory upon an analysis of 47 master's degree programs, and focused their analysis on departmental environments most conducive to teaching and learning. Delimited as it was, their model provides an excellent framework for examining the department as a whole, with all of its multiple missions. Recall that in our study of departmental assessment we found that engaged departments were one of five key attributes of a quality institutional climate. Our findings support Haworth and Conrad's, down to almost the last detail. Engaged departments have the following characteristics in common.

CHARACTERISTICS OF ENGAGED DEPARMENTS

An Atmosphere of Critical Inquiry

This quality underlies all the others. In Tierney (1999), organizational theorist Chris Argyris defines an "atmosphere of critical inquiry" as

> *[People] need to reflect critically on their own behavior, identify the ways they often inadvertently contribute to the organization's problems, and then change how they act. In particular, they must learn how the very way they go about defining and solving problems can be a source of problems in its own right.*

The preeminent contemporary thinker about how adults learn is Jack Mezirow. In a body of work dating back to the late 1970s, Mezirow has developed a theory of adult learning called "transformative learning." (For the latest on this theory see Mezirow and Associates, 1990). In brief, transformative learning operates from the large body of research on human cognition (cf., National Research Council, 2000), which suggests that people do not operate as blank slates, simply taking in information and storing it for later retrieval. Instead, people learn by constructing knowledge, organizing it into cognitive schema to which new information is then attached. Because everyone's life experience is totally unique, so then is the way in which we have constructed our knowledge of the world. Each of us treats new information differently. Sometimes new information which is not perceived as relevant given our existing schema is not retained at all. The older we become, the more resistant to change these schema are. Thus, Mezirow suggests, the only path to truly deep learning in adults is through transformation of these cognitive schema.

   A *disorienting dilemma*. This happens through what Mezirow calls a "disorienting dilemma," a problem which doesn't fit our current schema and thus forces us to see things differently. Only then, by revising our knowledge perspectives themselves, do we learn in more than just a superficial way. It's the difference between being able to recite the plot line of *Hamlet* and understanding the play in a way which helps us also to understand the timeless complexity of the human condition. It's the difference between appreciating the contributions of various world cultures and using those cultures as tools to help us better understand the assumptions underlying our own. And it's the difference between dismissing student complaints about a course's lack of relevance as simple immaturity and laziness and using students' comments as a trigger to cause us to reflect more critically on our own work.

   Discourse. The other key to transformative learning, according to Mezirow, is discourse. While deep learning may occur with individual reflection, it is much more likely, and much more likely to be powerful, when individuals begin to understand others' perspectives and how others experience the same reality differently. These conversations may themselves trigger disorienting dilemmas in the participants, leading to deeper shared understandings. The key is to avoid the sort of polarizing discourse in which the disorientation is so strong and anxiety-producing that participants simply retreat to their original positions, and don't learn anything at all (other than to avoid such situations in the future!). Instead, the goal is to create settings in which conflict is energizing in a positive way—a sort of constructive contention.

   As theoretical as this all is, it's easy to come up with common examples of how transformative learning works or doesn't work. The question is, how might it apply to departmental learning?

   Think for a moment about occasions in your own department that have lead to the kind of shared learning experience described above. If you're lucky you should be able to come up with several examples. What do they have in common? Ponder this question before reading further.

My guess is that your answer contains some or all of the following:

- People talked freely about their work.
- Collaboration was highly valued, with the belief that the whole would be greater than the sum of the parts.
- Self-disclosure was respected, valued, and encouraged, including self-disclosure about personal dilemmas and uncertainties.
- Departmental leaders took the initiative by modeling critical reflection and setting a reflective tone.
- An understanding prevailed in which there was no right answer, perspective, or approach; participants instead sought to learn from one another in an atmosphere of suspended prejudice.
- People understood that taking time for discourse was important and took priority over other tasks of the moment.
- The conversation did not prevent participants from making firm commitments to a course of action.

How does a departmental leader create such a climate? Part of the answer is implied in the above: by modeling critically reflective behavior personally and by creating settings where such reflection is comfortable. Brookfield (1995), however, suggests that creating a more reflective environment requires much more than rational argument or moral persuasion—it requires making changes in the social structure. He cites the following story told by Miles Horton, legendary adult educator and social activist:

> *One of Miles' favorite stories... was of a southern farmer who moved people to desegregated behavior not by the force of argument or appeals to compassion and democratic ideas, but by allowing only one drinking bucket in a field where whites and blacks were working or playing. If the white workers wanted to quench the thirst that had built up on a*

hot summer's day, they had to drink from the one barrel of water, using the one drinking ladle that had already touched the lips of the black workers. Miles claimed that the attitudinal shift produced when white workers drank from the same ladle as their black coworkers was far more profound and deep-seated than any resolution to change made in response to invocations of Christian ethics or social justice. (pp. 251-252)

Brookfield suggests two structural changes to the department:

1) Make a demonstrable commitment to critical reflection part of the reward system. This could take the form of criteria for hiring, asking students on course evaluation forms whether they were challenged or invited to examine other perspectives, and making portfolios a standard form of evidence for annual evaluations as well as for promotion and tenure.

2) Create professional development opportunities for faculty to engage in critical reflection, and make this part of what is considered to be good professional practice. Make time for critical conversation groups in the faculty workweek: "Every two to three weeks, part of the college day would be devoted to a troubleshooting session in which [faculty] would come together to talk about dilemmas and critical moments in their practice." (Brookfield, 1995, p. 253)

These are both useful ideas. To those who say they don't have time, or ask what they will be expected to do less of by engaging in more critical reflection as a department, my response would be, first, that reflection should be at the center of faculty work and not an add-on, and second, that careful deliberation as an academic community should make the collective job not only of higher quality but also more efficient. And here being efficient is a good thing.

A department which engages regularly in critical inquiry, therefore does the following (Preskill & Torres, 1998).

Asks open-ended questions about itself. In our study of departmental assessment (Wergin & Swingen, 2000), engaged departments regularly asked themselves deceptively-simple questions like, "What are we doing?" and, "Why are we doing it that way?" Usually these questions were raised within the context of a self-study (for accreditation or program review), which these departments used as an opportunity to raise some very basic issues about the collective work they were doing. Asking critical questions is usually not a problem for faculty. Faculty are, by nature and socialization, excellent at critique: We analyze and evaluate academic arguments because that's part of what scholarly inquiry is all about. But making these questions truly open-ended and phrasing them in a way that invites us to challenge our values, beliefs, and assumptions, is another matter altogether. The mental models we use to guide our behavior are powerful because they are implicit; we take them for granted as the way things are. Shaking loose these knowledge perspectives is a delicate art.

Reflects about what it does. Unfortunately, while faculty are often very good at asking critical questions, we are typically not very good at engaging in critical reflection. We reflect as part of our academic discipline, of course: we consider how ours and others' work expands and enriches the knowledge base of the field. But the sort of reflection described first by John Dewey (1933) and later by such writers as Brookfield (1995) and Mezirow (1990) is quite different from this. To Dewey and his proteges, true reflection consists of learning from our own behavior: examining our knowledge perspectives in light of our experiences, so that we might develop better understandings of how the world works. Thus we need to learn to reflect not just about what we know but also about how we use what we know to make decisions and guide our behavior. In other words, we need to reflect about the process as well as the content of the learning we do.

Shares individual reflections through dialogue. Mezirow (1990) argues that the only way for adults to engage in deep learning is to reflect in a way that allows participants to contrast their perspectives with others. As Preskill and Torres (1998) point out, dialogue requires an openness to diverse points of view and thus seeks to break new ground by sharing meanings, understanding the whole, and uncovering assumptions. As Massy, Wilger, and Colbeck (1994) so clearly discovered, this sort of dialogue rarely happens in academic departments, where—if issues are discussed at all—the intent is to inform or persuade, not to reflect together. When, on the other hand, the purpose of the dialogue is to learn from one another, disagreement becomes a source of energy for learning.

Makes meaning of the data it collects. In Chapter 3, I reported how rare it is for institutions or their academic units to go beyond a simple analysis of data and to have an open discussion about what the data mean. Most seem to assume that data speak for themselves and that interpreting the data should be straightforward and should lead to a singular conclusion. Technology has made information so accessible that institutions can become buried in it. Departments characterized by a culture of inquiry, on the other hand, ask themselves, "What are the issues we face as a department? What kind of information would help us sort out these issues and become more informed about alternative courses of action?" And, "Once we have the information in hand, how will we interpret it?"

Here's an example. A biology department at one of the institutions we visited for the departmental assessment study (Wergin & Swingen, 2000) was interested in how well it was preparing its majors for careers in the health professions. Among the data it collected were attrition rates for various health science schools, and the department discovered that graduates who entered schools of nursing or physical therapy dropped out at much higher rates than those who attended schools of medicine or dentistry. "What do we make of this?," faculty wanted to know. "Does this mean we aren't doing the job we should to prepare students for nursing and allied health professions?" (As it turned out, further investigation revealed that the attrition rates at these schools reflected attrition for all students, not just their ex-majors.)

Connects reflection with action. John Dewey was right: People do learn most deeply when they both reflect and act on their learning. Departments characterized by a culture of critical inquiry ask themselves, "Given what we now know, what should we be doing differently?"

Coming up with an appropriate answer to that question involves what Judith Ramaley (1999, personal communication) has called the "management of reasonable risk": that is, supporting initiatives that will help move the unit along, but not making them such high-stakes exercises that failure would be catastrophic. Usually this requires that departments take good ideas, pilot them carefully, give them a chance to work, and agree up front about what evidence will be most helpful in gauging success and making changes.

A Shared Understanding of Faculty Work

As I've suggested earlier, in an increasingly privatized academic culture, faculty need all the more to feel connected to an intellectual community. Connection—beyond the superficial connections of the "hollowed collegium" (Massy, Wilger, & Colbeck, 1994), anyway—requires that faculty members have a shared knowledge of the work they do. Colleges and universities are designed in ways that seem almost guaranteed to reduce interaction among the faculty, however. Bill Tierney puts it well: "The faculty are housed in insular disciplinary structures that exacerbate, rather than stimulate, the ability to communicate across differences. A paradox exists in that, at a time of increasing interdisciplinarity, ...we work in structures and study areas that decrease collegial bonds and understandings" (1999, p. 11).

To be sure, much of what faculty do is solitary, and that won't change. And I won't go so far as to suggest, as some have, that faculty workspaces be redesigned so that they do their solitary work at home and spend their time at the university interacting with students and colleagues! I'm also not suggesting that shared understanding can be gained only by having faculty members spend more time in meetings. While dialogue is an important, even necessary, element of critical reflection, there are other ways to accomplish shared understanding.

Faculty work is community property. First, the department begins with the premise that faculty work (teaching and service as well as scholarship) is community property (Shulman, 1995)—that faculty work is regarded as part of the work of the department, and thus is open to peer collaboration and peer review. Both my own research (Wergin & Swingen, 2000) and that of the Faculty Work Project of the Associated New American Colleges (McMillin & Berberet, 2002) show quite clearly that any attempt at defining unit mission and collective responsibility is an empty exercise without this understanding. This means that faculty have no proprietary rights on courses or programs; that faculty visitation in one another's classes is acceptable, even routine; that faculty members make curricular decisions based on a solid knowledge of what is taught and how; that service commitments are made and negotiated communally, as part of an understanding of how the department's interests are to be served; and that individual faculty workplans, including goals, expectations, and evaluation criteria, are public to departmental faculty.

Accepts that priorities are not always clear. Second, the department acknowledges that under the current structure of most institutions, faculty will be pulled in multiple directions, with little guidance—or worse, mixed messages—about how to assign priorities. The burden is greatest on junior faculty, who often find themselves feeling as if they have to do it all. In addition, faculty aren't aware at times of collaborative opportunities, or ways in which their work may be duplicative, or even at cross-purposes, with others. The message to the department should be this: The days of the "Lone Ranger of the Intellect" (Langenburg, 1992) are long gone, if in fact they ever existed. The increasing, and increasingly diverse, demands on faculty require a negotiation of priorities at the unit level.

Faculty have a vehicle for sharing their work. Third, faculty develop a forum for sharing their work in a way that builds trust and provides assurances that no individual sweetheart deals have been struck with the chair. There are several ways to do this. At one university an ad hoc faculty group created an inventory outlining the range of faculty tasks and duties and used the findings to create a visual representation in the form of a faculty work diagram which was then used as a rubric for individual departments to identify how the workload breaks down among individual faculty and where each of them is focusing effort (McMillin & Berberet, 2002). In this way faculty have been able to locate where their contributions fit within the larger work of the department and where, in turn, their department contributes to the work of the institution. At another university the work of the department was defined in a two-day off-campus retreat, where I broke participants into program groups and asked each one to identify their collective work, how they felt their work contributed to that of the department, and then how they saw the contribution of other program groups. This exercise led to clearer perspectives of faculty roles and cleared up long-term misunderstandings. I've been struck at how powerfully going public with individual faculty work creates both an atmosphere of trust and a heightened sense of individual accountability.

A Shared Sense of Mission and Collective (Collegial) Responsibility

The central point here is that an understanding of collective faculty work must start with the individual and work outward, not the other way around. Departmental discussions about mission are virtually guaranteed to make faculty eyes roll to the back of their heads, and why shouldn't they? This is just the sort of activity that drives faculty crazy: Not only does it lack intellectual stimulation, it's also widely perceived—usually accurately—as an empty exercise that will have little utility beyond satisfying some administrative mandate or other. Besides, faculty members are so good at deconstructing text that language will be sliced and diced to the point where the mission statement really doesn't communicate anything unique about the department (Seymour, 1992).

There's a better way, and that's to work from the inside out. A shared sense of mission must begin with an inventory of the work faculty do, as suggested above, and then an examination of what this work adds up to and how the collective whole adds value to the institution. As McMillin and her colleagues point out: "Collective work is not the same as aggregate work. The work of an academic unit is more than the sum total of what its faculty do: It is a negotiated understanding of how the work of the unit as a whole fits within the larger mission of the institution" (McMillin & Berberet, 2002, p. 94). Further, they suggest, the fit between individual faculty and their departments, and between departments and their institutions, should be described in terms of adding value, or "enabling or contributing to the work of others" (p. 95). The authors, as spokespersons for faculty teams engaged in the Faculty Work Project sponsored by the Associated New American Colleges, propose a simple but compelling "circle of value," which they describe this way:

> *Individual faculty structure their particular work experiences to pursue their specific interests, skills, and talents but in the context of identifying the ways in which their work adds value to that of the academic unit to which they belong. Similarly the work of the unit, as a collective, must add value to the work of the institution... Finally, to complete this circle, the institution must also add value to the work of the faculty... Thus, it becomes the obligation of all members of the institution—faculty, staff, and administrators—to add value or contribute to the whole. (p. 95)*

As the authors acknowledge, the circle of value is not a closed system that ignores relationships outside the circle (such as those faculty might have with their disciplinary communities), or joint responsibilities that academic units might share with others. But it does represent a useful perspective, a point of departure, and a way to center departmental conversation.

So how, then, to shift the focus from an aggregate to a collective notion of faculty work at the departmental level? Once an inventory of individual faculty work is complete, how should this negotiation work? In particular, how might the department deal with the difficult question of what to do less of?

Define "collective." First it's important to clarify the meaning of "collective," a term that to some may have unfortunate political connotations. I use the term, however, in the same way that John Bennett refers to the healthy academic "collegium," where "individuals achieve maximum freedom and personal satisfaction...[including] the feeling that one is part of something greater than oneself" (1998, p. 30); or in the same way that Joseph Katz refers to the academic "community" which

> *should be a community of persons united by collective under-*
> *standings, by common and communal goals, by a bond of*
> *reciprocal obligation, and by a flow of sentiment which*
> *makes the preservation of the community an object of desire,*
> *not merely a matter of prudence or a command of duty.*
> *Community implies a form of social obligation governed by*
> *principles different from those operative in the marketplace*
> *and the state. (quoted in Tierney, 1999, pp. 11-12)*

And so when I use the term "collective responsibility" I mean that the academic unit as a whole accepts responsibility for what it does and the impact it has. It functions in a way that promotes both individual and mutual accountability. Collective responsibility thus requires meaningful faculty collaboration: work engaged in by people with complementary skills who are committed to a common purpose and who feel responsible for the collective product. This notion of collaboration requires more than what is normally found in a faculty working group, where people contribute to a shared purpose but feel responsible only for what they have contributed individually. It's important to understand also, however, that in academic settings "collaboration" doesn't always have to mean "teamwork." Bensimon and O'Neill (1998) have suggested a helpful distinction between two kinds of collaboration: "group-organization collaboration" is what we normally think of as collaboration, namely having groups of people work together for a common purpose. The authors also suggest however that "individual-organization collaboration," people working *individually* toward a mutually-understood goal, is equally valuable and in some ways a better fit to the culture of the academy.

Develop departmental goals. Once the department takes inventory of individual faculty work, therefore, and has ascertained the points of commonality, the next step is to abstract from these individual aspirations to a set of implicit departmental goals. The department needs to ask some fundamental questions of itself: What do we add up to as a unit? How are we more than just an aggregate of individual faculty activity? What is it about our collective strengths, interests, and experience that makes our group unique, different from similar departments in other universities? How might we best contribute to the good of our students, our institution, and our discipline?

We must be careful not to assume that everyone's work will fit neatly into a conceptual box. Academic departments (and the larger institutions that they're part of) have diffuse purposes; they vary widely in the interdependence of their members; they usually do not have clear tasks that all members share. Trying to turn academic departments into teams, therefore, is a losing proposition. Instead, the departmental mission which evolves inductively from individual inventory and collective reflection is an anchor, a touchstone, a point of connection for all department members. It's the point at which faculty members can identify how they might have the greatest impact, and conversely which activities they might de-emphasize.

Differentiated Faculty Work

This step is critical—and also extraordinarily difficult. It is critical because it makes little sense to go to the trouble of defining the work of the department without taking the additional step of matching the department's work to individual talents and interests. It is difficult because the cultural prescriptions of the academy continue to point in the opposite direction:

- The system continues to reward star achievers with differential achievement, mobility, prestige, and salary. This wouldn't be a problem if there were multiple routes to academic stardom, but we all know better. Fairweather (1996) showed that even in so-called teaching institutions, like liberal arts colleges, it's scholarship, not teaching or service, that counts.
- Departments can't do this alone. They will have little incentive to make radical changes in their processes if the dominant perception is that the rest of the university—

or the discipline for that matter—continues to reward the status quo. There is ample evidence that the further departments venture toward the fringes, the more nervous faculty become about negative consequences (Wergin, 1994). Why should faculty want to make changes to their roles if the rewards will stay the same?

- Like any other systemic change in the academy, implementation is difficult, the time investment is great, and positive returns may be slow in coming.

A dramatic illustration of this latter point is provided by an in-depth case study of faculty work differentiation at a major state university (Pruett, 2001). Pruett studied how a university-wide policy promulgating faculty differentiation at the departmental level was actually implemented in four arts and sciences departments. She found the implementation to be extraordinarily diverse. One department had full implementation: Faculty members shared their work freely and negotiated differential assignments on an annual basis; another implemented the policy on paper, but faculty kept doing what they were doing anyway; a third implemented the policy only for nonproductive (read nonpublishing) faculty as a way to force them to do more teaching; and the fourth did not implement the policy at all, and even constructed dummy files to make it look as if they had!

Individualized faculty work plans. The key to the success of differentiated work lies in individualized faculty workplans. Workplans have two purposes: 1) They provide a framework for individual faculty activity within the context of departmental mission and goals; and 2) Collectively, they represent the mosaic of the department's work as a whole and for what it proposes to be individually and mutually accountable. As McMillin and her colleagues point out, a balance needs to be struck between defining boundaries and maintaining flexibility:

> *Institutions will have to decide just how differentiated such work plans can be. Some parameters may be set on a campus-wide or unit-wide basis, that is, the minimum/ maximum percentage of weight faculty may place on citizenship, scholarship, or teaching in evaluation. Some parameters may be set by*

the contract status or career stage of a particular faculty member; that is, probationary faculty might need to attend more to teaching and research than citizenship; faculty on part-time or visiting contracts might have limited student advising or service commitments. However, the greater the flexibility given to the faculty of a unit to negotiate their plans collaboratively, the more creative possibilities that can be generated... Overall, we would encourage institutions to minimize boundaries and maximize flexibility. One size does not have to fit all units any more than all individual faculty. (McMillin & Berberet, 2002, pp. 98-99).

One additional point needs to be made about faculty workplans: Their use cannot be allowed to devolve into just another administrative chore, because to do so would defeat their whole purpose. They need to be living documents, always available for renegotiation as circumstances and opportunities dictate. Further, it's critical that workplans recognize not only the diversity of skills and interests across departmental faculty, but also the diversity of skills and interests across a single faculty member's career. Stereotyping a colleague as someone who teaches the intro course or handles university governance or gets the grants is unfair both to the faculty member and to the department. Vibrancy cannot be maintained unless people are encouraged to grow and try new things.

The McMillin and Berberet (2002) volume, *A New Academic Compact,* contains several examples of useful ways departments have found to develop and carry out policies of faculty differentiation, and the reader is invited to peruse them for ideas. What's most striking about these examples is how different they are: There's no one best way to do it. The key is in finding ways of working together that make sense for the kind of department you have.

A Shared Understanding of How the Department Adds Value to the Institution

Departments add value—that is, they contribute to the good of the institution—in vastly different ways. Criteria that make sense for a biology department with a significant research agenda and substantial service courses will make no sense at all for a music department with small enrollments and zero grant support. These departments contribute in totally different ways to the common good of the institution and thus need to be evaluated accordingly. Measures of value added by the biology department might include the traditional ones: credit hours generated, external grant income, and the like. The music department, on the other hand, with an emphasis on professional skill development and contributions to the cultural life of the community, will likely have to rely on softer forms of evidence, such as placements of graduates and reputational and testimonial data.

Still, the temptation is great to measure what is easiest to measure, and to come up with quantifiable criteria by which departments may be compared. The worst strategy for a department is to be passive about this and to accept whatever criteria are proposed externally. Even with complicated formulas to help account for departmental differences in class size, studio or lab emphasis, or investment in distance learning, no single criterion or set of criteria can possibly capture a department's value to the institution, and it is up to the departmental faculty, speaking as a collective, to propose how they wish to be assessed. Faculty are the only ones who are able to identify the nuances of the work they do and the impact it has. Hence, questions such as these should also be asked as part of critical reflection: "How do we know that we are successfully accomplishing our mission? What evidence would help us determine how effectively we are accomplishing our teaching, service, and scholarship goals? How might we demonstrate ways in which we add value to the institution? How might we use information to better advance our agenda?" And so on. My experience in working with departments, deans, and central administration on these issues suggests a widespread acknowledgment of the strength of departmental diversity, and a willingness to negotiate criteria for evaluating the work of the department. The key is whether the department is proactive about this, and is willing to step forward and say, "This is how we add value to the institution"... and "This is the sort of evidence which will show it."

CONCLUSION: THE ENGAGED DEPARTMENT

I've summarized the key themes of my argument in Figure 4.1.

FIGURE 4.1
THE ENGAGED DEPARTMENT

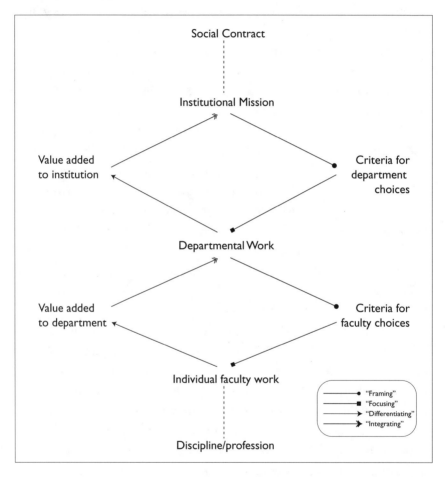

Academic work may be defined at three levels: 1) work of the individual faculty member, 2) work of the department, and 3) work of the school/institution. The work of the department is, rightly, at the center of this double hexagon. Departmental work is defined in two ways: by the collective work of individual faculty, defined in terms of how faculty add value to the department, and by negotiation with the institution, defined in terms of how the department itself adds value. Institutional priorities become criteria for departmental choices, and departmental priorities become criteria for faculty choices. Throughout all this, four different processes are going on, reflected in the four directional arrows. The arrows pointing southeast and southwest indicate, respectively, framing and focusing processes: identifying the options and criteria available, and using these criteria to make decisions about where to put the energy. The arrows pointing northwest and northeast indicate, respectively, differentiating and integrating processes: recognizing how contributions to the collective good can take multiple forms and using these differential contributions to define a more coherent whole. Individual faculty work is also influenced by the respective discipline or profession, and institutional work is also influenced by its social contract.

In my view, a quality department takes all of these processes and influences seriously and reflects critically about itself as it makes judgments of value. Another way of thinking about this is that a quality department has two sides: It not only frames choices according to institutional fit and its collective strengths; it evaluates itself the same way. An engaged department, therefore, behaves in ways consistent with the following principles:

Principles of the Engaged Department

1) The work of the institution, defined in terms of its social compact and the collective work of its departmental units, frames the choices for departmental work.

2) The department is guided both by the aggregate work of its member faculty, and by how it adds value as a whole to the institution.

3) The work of the department provides a basis for framing the work individual faculty members do.

4) Faculty members are guided in their choices both by how they add value to their disciplines and how they add value to the work of their departments.

5) Choices, whether made by individual faculty members or by departments as a whole, are the product of negotiation with key stakeholders.

Proactive approaches to quality require that department members address two matters they rarely address: the shared values upon which the work of the department rests, and the kind of evidence that will help them make the most useful judgments of quality. I'll take these issues up in the next two chapters.

REFERENCES

Association of American Colleges and Universities. (1985). *Integrity in the college curriculum: A report to the academic community.* Washington, DC: Author.

American Association of University Professors. (1940, 1995). *AAUP policy documents and reports.* Washington, DC: author.

Alpert, D. (1986). Performance and paralysis: The organizational context of the American research university. *Journal of Higher Education, 56* (3), 76-102.

Bennett, J. B. (1998). *Collegial professionalism : The academy, individualism, and the common good.* Phoenix, AZ: Oryx.

Bensimon, E. M., & Neumann, A. (1993). *Redesigning collegiate leadership: Teams and teamwork in higher education.* Baltimore, MD: Johns Hopkins University Press.

Bensimon, E. M., & O'Neill, H. F., Jr. (1998). Collaborative effort to measure faculty work. *Liberal Education, 84* (4).

Brookfield, S. D. (1995). *Becoming a critically reflective teacher.* San Francisco, CA: Jossey-Bass.

Clark, B. R. (1987). *The academic life: Small worlds, different worlds.* Princeton, NJ: Carnegie Foundation for the Advancement of Teaching.

Dewey, J. (1933). *How we think: A restatement of the relation of reflective thinking to the educative process.* Lexington, MA: D. C. Heath.

Fairweather, J. (1996). *Faculty work and the public trust: Restoring the value of teaching and public service in American academic life.* Boston, MA: Allyn & Bacon.

Haworth, J. G., & Conrad, C. F. (1997). *Emblems of quality in higher education: Developing and sustaining high-quality programs.* Needham Heights, MA: Allyn & Bacon.

Langenburg, D. N. (1992, September 2). Team scholarship could help strengthen scholarly traditions. *The Chronicle of Higher Education,* A64.

Massy, W. F., Wilger, A. K., & Colbeck, C. (1994, July/August). Overcoming "hollowed" collegiality. *Change, 26* (4), 10-20.

McMillin, L. A., & Berberet, J. (Eds.). (2002) *A new academic compact: Revisioning the relationship between faculty and their institutions.* Bolton, MA: Anker.

Mezirow, J. (1990). How critical reflection triggers transformative learning. In J. Mezirow & Associates (Eds.), *Fostering critical reflection in adulthood: A guide to transformative and emancipatory learning.* San Francisco, CA: Jossey-Bass.

National Research Council. (2000). *How people learn: Brain, mind, experience, and school* (expanded ed.). Washington, DC: National Academy Press.

Preskill, H., & Torres, R. T. (1998). *Evaluative inquiry for learning in organizations.* Thousand Oaks, CA: Sage.

Pruett, E. S. (2001). *Restructuring faculty workload: A qualitative study of the effects of faculty role differentiation on senior faculty members' perception of the quality of their work lives.* Doctoral dissertation, Virginia Commonwealth University.

Rice, R. E. (1996). Making a place for the new American scholar. *New pathways: Faculty career and employment for the 21st century.* Working Paper Series, Inquiry No. 1. Washington, DC: AAHE.

Schuster, J. H., Wheeler, D. W., & Associates (1990). *Enhancing faculty careers: Strategies for development and renewal.* San Francisco, CA: Jossey-Bass.

Senge, P. M. (2000). The academy as learning community: Contradiction in terms or realizable future? In A. F. Lucas & Associates (Eds.), *Leading academic change: Essential roles for department chairs* (pp. 275-300). San Francisco, CA: Jossey-Bass.

Seymour, D. T. (1992). *On Q: Causing quality in higher education.* Phoenix, AZ: Oryx.

Shulman, L. (1995, January). *Teaching as community property.* Address to AAHE Forum on Faculty Roles and Rewards, San Diego, CA.

Tierney, W. G. (1999). *Building the responsive campus: Creating high performance colleges and universities.* Thousand Oaks, CA: Sage.

Tompkins, J. P. (1992, November/December). The way we live now. *Change, 24,* 12-19.

United States Office of Scientific Research and Development. (1945). *Science, the endless frontier: A report to the President by Vannevar Bush.* Washington, DC: Author.

University of California at Los Angeles Higher Education Research Institute. (1997). *The American college teacher: National norms for the 1995-96 HERI faculty survey.* Los Angeles, CA: author.

Walvoord, B. E., Carey, A. K., Smith, H. L., Soled, S. W., Way, P. K., & Zorn, D. (2000). *Academic departments: How they work, how they change.* ASHE-ERIC Higher Education Report, 27 (8). San Francisco, CA: Jossey-Bass.

Wergin, J. F. (1994). *The collaborative department: How five campuses are inching toward cultures of collective responsibility.* Washington, DC: AAHE.

Wergin, J. F., & Swingen, J. N. (2000). *Departmental assessment: How some colleges are effectively evaluating the collective work of faculty.* Washington, DC: AAHE.

NEGOTIATING DEPARTMENTAL VALUES

We don't see the world as it is. We see

it as we are.

—Anais Nin

INTRODUCTION

Making decisions about quality, by definition, means making judgments about value. Value judgments range from defining which evaluation questions are worth asking, to delineating the kinds and sources of evidence that might be helpful, to making sense of the data we collect and deciding what to do. Before I take up the topics of question-asking, evidence-collecting, and meaning-making, I want to discuss how a department might define for itself more effectively those core values upon which such decisions will ultimately rest. As Donald Kennedy, former president of Stanford, noted, "The fact that most institutional decisions represent, in the end, the collective values and aspirations of the faculty helps to explain why universities are organized the way they are and behave as they do" (quoted in Walvoord et al., 2000, p. 15). In this chapter I'll argue that a quality department has a set of core values which have been negotiated with key department stakeholders.

How many times have you participated in discussions that proceeded from statements like the following?

> *Enrollment trends in our major are down, and we need to do something about it.*

> *Students are complaining about the senior seminar being too hard. How did we get such a bunch of crybabies?*

> *We've had a productive year—a record number of single-authored publications in refereed journals.*

> *Our graduate students seem content to land academic jobs in second- and third-tier institutions. Where have we failed?*

Notice what's going on in each of these statements. Each contains a set of implicit assumptions about what the data mean and what should be done. In the first, a drop in enrollment is taken as evidence that a problem exists, that the problem is something the department can do something about, and that a way needs to be found to reverse the decline. In the second, student complaints are taken as evidence that something is wrong with the students themselves, not the course or the teaching, and that the department needs to recruit a better, more motivated crop. In the third, departmental publications are taken as evidence of scholarly productivity, with the clear implication that more is better. And in the fourth, students' finding academic positions in institutions other than research universities is taken as evidence of a weak graduate program. I'm not suggesting that none of these arguments has merit. I am suggesting that each one depends on inferences based on assumed truths, each of which in turn is open to multiple interpretations.

Let's look at the last statement, for example. (Those readers in non-research universities may find the position articulated there ridiculous or even insulting, but those of you in graduate programs know what I'm talking about.) Graduate faculty everywhere have long used the prestige of universities that hire their doctoral students as benchmarks of their own success as faculty mentors: If their students land in more prestigious institutions, great; if they go to a comparable institution, OK; if they wind up at a "lesser" university, not so good; and if they choose to teach in a non-selective baccalaureate institution or a community college, well, that would just not be acceptable. (Not to mention having a graduate opt out of academic life entirely!) This line of reasoning makes perfect sense when you deconstruct the logic and understand the implicit standards being used. It goes like this: Institutions can be ranked for prestige along unidimensional scales of quality, and since these rankings are widely accepted, the quality of a graduate can be measured by the quality of the institution which selects that person as a faculty member. Further, students should want to follow in their mentors' footsteps and teach in a research university, the more prestigious the better. If students don't want that, or if they strive for a position in a research university and settle for something less, then it's a negative reflection on the graduate program, and on the mentor personally. To the graduate faculty these truths are standards against which perceptions and experiences are compared, and value judgments about program quality made.

But others, those with a different stake in the department, might make different interpretations entirely. Graduate students have different standards of value. For many of them, a quality graduate department is one which prepares them for a range of potential professional careers, and so diversity in job placement is a positive sign, not a negative one. Furthermore, students are increasingly looking for careers that are different in kind from those of their mentors—careers which offer a greater potential for integration with their personal lives (Trower, Austin, & Sorcinelli, 2001). For many of these students, teaching in a community college would be a career of choice, not of default. Finally, those institutions which hire fresh PhDs for faculty jobs would likely be gratified to see a graduate department take steps to prepare its students for a broader range of faculty responsibilities, as the national Preparing Future Faculty Program has convincingly shown (Gaff, Pruitt-Logan, Weibl, & Associates, 2000).

QUALITY IS IN THE EYE OF THE BEHOLDER

I use this extended example to argue that when it comes to departmental quality, quality is truly in the eye of the beholder. Acknowledging and understanding this is absolutely necessary if a department is to get anywhere with enhancing quality. I don't want to imply that every discussion about academic quality is doomed to become mired in relativism, or that full consensus is necessary. In the example above, graduate faculty, graduate students, and institutions hiring these students for academic jobs all have different interests, and thus will view program quality in those terms. Graduate faculty's interests are to replicate themselves and send these academic clones off to places of high prestige, where they will reflect positively on both the institution and themselves. Students' interests are to gain a professional credential that is marketable in ways that fit their life goals. Faculty at hiring institutions have an interest in attracting students from programs which best prepare them for academic work at places like theirs. Different interests are being served in each case, but do they conflict? No, not necessarily, not unless one set is used to the exclusion of the others. Adhering to values dictated by only one stakeholder group will almost always lead to trouble.

For many years, quality graduate programs were those which had faculty with national or international reputations, a substantial track record in grant support for research, and a highly competitive base of student applicants. (The National Research Council, by the way, still rates graduate programs this way.) Thus, it made sense for graduate faculty to gauge their success by placement in big-name universities; students wanted to go to these universities because they would have a better chance of getting a prestigious faculty appointment; and hiring institutions would judge the caliber of their faculty on the basis of where they obtained their graduate degrees. But look at what's happened: The bottom fell out of the academic job market for most disciplines in the 1980s, resulting in a buyer's market among hiring institutions. These institutions were also feeling pressure to pay more attention to teaching and engagement with the community. The result was that search committees began looking more critically at applicants' credentials: not just their research records, but also their potential for contributing to a broader set of institutional goals. Students, realizing that they weren't being prepared adequately for the vast majority of academic positions available, began to lobby for change and to seek out those graduate programs which might better prepare them for careers in smaller universities, liberal arts colleges, and community colleges. Many of the provider institutions, in turn, have developed Preparing Future Faculty programs and marketed them heavily. In their eyes, program quality has taken on a whole new meaning.

What's to be learned from this? Not just that quality depends on the frame of reference held by those with different and often conflicting interests, but also that it's possible to draw upon these differences and negotiate them in a way that will lead to a better program, one which will more closely match stakeholder needs.

NEGOTIATION: A DEFINITION

I want to be clear about what I mean by "negotiation." The usual connotation of the term suggests compromise, like a buyer and seller haggling over the price of a car. But in practice, negotiation has a much broader meaning: Negotiation occurs whenever people with different sets of interests engage in discussion for the purpose of reaching agreement. The interests people have represent the stakes they have in the program. Graduate students have an interest in getting the academic job they want; institutions which hire them have an interest in finding candidates who will give them the best mix of talent for their institutional needs; and graduate faculty have an interest in producing graduates who will enhance their and their departments' prestige. Cervero and Wilson (1994) have suggested that educational programs are never neutral activities, but represent an expression of interests about how the world ought to be. Educators' central responsibility, they note, is therefore to be clear about "what kind of world they want their practice to shape" (p. 5).

I agree completely. A central responsibility of academic departments is, first, to be clear about whose interests and values are at stake and how they may be brought to the table, and second, to negotiate these interests into a set of quality standards for which the department is willing to be held collectively responsible.

HOW TO NEGOTIATE INTERESTS

Some excellent guidance is available for doing this. In their book *Fourth Generation Evaluation* (1989), Egon Guba and Yvonna Lincoln describe the act of program evaluation as much more than mere science, or getting the facts. Such a perspective assumes the existence of an objective truth out there somewhere, and so our task is to find a way to identify it and measure it. Guba and Lincoln's view, instead, is that evaluation is the result of stakeholders attempting to make meaning of what they observe, that it is a form of constructed reality which is influenced enormously by stakeholders' own values. Hence, different stakeholder groups will interpret the same set of facts in different ways.

In addition to Guba and Lincoln's model I'll draw upon three other sources extensively. First is Cervero and Wilson's *Planning Responsibly for Adult Education* (1994), second is McMillin and Berberet's *A New Academic Compact* (2002), and third is an article I wrote many years ago on evaluating organizational policy making (Wergin, 1976). I have taken the perspectives from these three sources and pulled them together in a way that is based on my own experience in working with academic departments. The approach I recommend for negotiating departmental standards has six steps.

Identify the Program or Department's Stakeholders

The term "stakeholder" is being used so often today that it's in danger of becoming a hackneyed cliché like "customer." But quite simply, a stakeholder is anyone who stands to gain or lose by what the program does, and so has a vested interest in it. Guba and Lincoln (1989) identify three kinds of stakeholders: *"agents,* those persons involved in producing, using, or implementing [the program]; *beneficiaries,* those persons who profit in some way from [the program]; and *victims,* those persons who are negatively affected by [the program]" (pp. 201-202).

The principal stakeholders for an academic department should not be hard to identify. Agents would include the departmental faculty and chair; beneficiaries would include students, alumni, parents, employers, the academic discipline, and the university administration (at least in theory!). Identifying victims isn't nearly so obvious, but in an academic context these would include other academic departments who stand to lose resources if favor is shown to the department in question. While conceivably all of society is potentially a beneficiary or victim of the program, for our purposes it's sufficient to include only those whose stakes in the program are relatively high.

Engage in Responsive Focusing With Each Stakeholder Group, Beginning in the Center With the Departmental Faculty and Working Outward

Responsive focusing (Guba & Lincoln, 1989) is a way of defining what the negotiation of standards will be about, and it identifies three kinds of assertions held by stakeholders: Claims are assertions which are favorable to the program; concerns are assertions which are unfavorable to the program; and issues are assertions about which reasonable people might disagree. Because different stakeholder groups will hold different sets of claims, concerns, and issues, it's important up front to identify these as points of departure and put them on the table. Here's how this might be done. I've tried this approach as a consultant to departments in several universities, and it works.

Define faculty interests. For the agents of the department, namely its faculty, engage in a focused discussion (electronically; or better, in a faculty meeting or series of meetings) for the purpose of defining the faculty's collective interests. Ask several straightforward questions: "What are the strengths of this department? What is it doing that is good? How does it add value to the school and the institution" (McMillin & Berberet, 2002)? And, "What are its weaknesses? What is it doing that it shouldn't be doing? What isn't it doing that it should?" Group responses into the three categories of claims, concerns, and issues, and share these with the faculty for comment.

- **Claims** represent shared values about which little negotiation is needed, and thus form the core of quality standards as seen by departmental faculty. Possible claims
  include, "The department provides a fertile environment
  for faculty scholarship"; "Students are prepared fully for
  certification as (nurses, accountants, engineers, etc.)";
  "Students get a firm foundation in X discipline, regardless
  of major." Note that while statements like these may
  resemble formal departmental goals or mission statements, their source is not a set of lofty abstractions but values held by individuals. They are also all value judgments.
- **Concerns** also represent shared values, but ones which
  faculty feel are not being well served. Possible concerns
  include, "We are not well respected by other departments
  in the school for our contributions"; "There's an imbalance
  in the reward system which favors research over teaching";
  "Faculty are fragmented and isolated from one another."
  These add to the core of quality standards, the implication
  being that addressing the concerns will enhance departmental quality.
- **Issues,** or clear and reasonable differences, will form the
  basis of the most intense negotiation. Examples of issues
  would include disagreement on admissions policies, promotion and tenure criteria, or faculty workload policies.

List consensus values. Develop a list of consensus values, based
on both claims and concerns, with the concerns expressed in positive
terms. For example, instead of saying, "Faculty are fragmented and isolated from one another," change the wording to say, "Faculty have substantial knowledge of each others' work, and collaborate frequently."

Examine the issues. Decide first which issues are worth worrying
about. Ask, "What will be the consequences to us of not doing anything
about this particular disagreement?" If the answer is "little or nothing,"
then the appropriate course is simply to agree to disagree.
Departmental faculty will disagree on many things that are only related

tangentially to core values and, thus, departmental quality. For example, a departmental issue may revolve around what the department's research priorities should be. As long as individual faculty are productive, and their personal priorities don't conflict, then resolution of this issue may not be critical. But if the issue does reflect core values then the disagreement will have to be negotiated. One such issue might be faculty roles and responsibilities. Some of the faculty might argue that in a quality department, all faculty engage in active scholarship; others might contend that faculty contributions could take many forms, and that as long as the department as a whole engages in active scholarship, members should be expected to contribute in differential ways, namely by focusing on teaching or service. Negotiating these value differences might lead to an agreement that departmental "quality" requires each faculty member to be actively engaged intellectually with the discipline in ways which contribute to one of the four scholarships defined in *Scholarship Reconsidered* (Boyer, 1990), but that not all faculty are expected to be equally productive in scholarship, as long as they are able to add value in other ways.

Get feedback from others. Use the faculty's program values as stimuli to sound out departmental beneficiaries, beginning with those closest to the department, namely students, alumni, and the next level of administration (dean). Say: "This is what our department stands for, the values by which we propose the quality of our work to be judged. How would your standards be different, if at all?" And, "How do you think the department adds value to the school (institution)? How do you think it should add value in ways it doesn't at present?"

Pull Together the Claims, Concerns, and Issues From the Stakeholder Groups and Sort Them by Strength of Interest

Here the purpose is to sort through the values held by those outside the department and to put some clear choices before departmental faculty. In the academy, like other professional organizations, academic departments are semi-autonomous units and hold most of the cards. Their faculty determine, within limits, how they will approach their jobs and spend their time, and the department as a whole determines, within limits, where it will put its resources and how it will respond to various institutional initiatives and guidelines. Thus, it would be neither realistic nor even desirable to engage in a process of values negotiation by pretending that all parties to the table had equal power to influence the outcome. At the same time it would be a huge mistake to assume complete departmental autonomy, as if none of the other stakeholder interests mattered. And so in practice departmental values will be central, with other stakeholders' values reflected against them. One might think of the key players as shown in Figure 5.1.

FIGURE 5.1
STAKEHOLDERS' CIRCLES

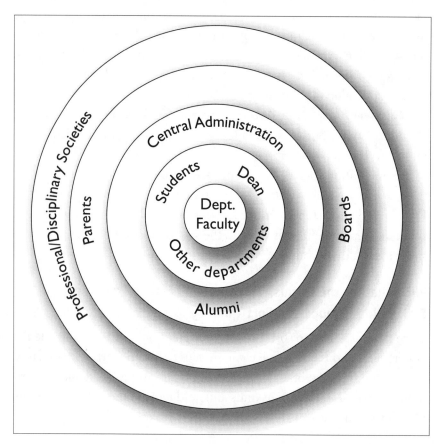

Faculty and the chair are in the center of a series of concentric circles. In the first ring of stakeholders are students, other departments in the school having close curricular or scholarly ties, and the dean; in the second ring are the central academic administration of the institution and alumni; in the third ring are parents and the institution's board; and in the fourth ring is the disciplinary/professional society to which the department belongs. Other key stakeholders and their position will depend on the department's mission. For example, departments with strong community ties through service-learning and other engagement projects will likely put these interests on one of the inner circles. The closer to the center, the stronger the accountability, and thus the more critical the interests. For each stakeholder group, as with departmental faculty, synthesize claims and concerns into shared values. Within-stakeholder issues may be put aside for the moment, but into a "bears watching" category.

Compare Faculty Standards With Those of Other Stakeholders, Starting With Those Most Central to the Department, and Identify Discrepancies

These differences represent different notions of quality. They are neither good nor bad, right nor wrong. They will, however, have to be negotiated, most particularly those near the center. How the department chooses to do this is what makes the process so consciously political.

Choose a Negotiating Position, Based on the Real or Potential Power of the Stakeholder or Stakeholder Group

The department has several options available: competition, bargaining, co-optation, and coalition (Wergin, 1976). These are arranged in order of highest to lowest risk, and least to most loss of autonomy.

Competition. A competitive strategy is simply to ignore the difference, or to attempt to educate or persuade the other that the conflict should be resolved in favor of the dominant interest. For example, the department might take a competitive stance against student interests in reducing the curricular emphasis on liberal learning in favor of a more technical orientation, by taking pains to explain and justify the importance of a liberal education.

Bargaining. A bargaining strategy is the familiar spirit of compromise, where each side softens its position until agreement is reached. A department might bargain with its dean, who wants more of an emphasis on research grants as a standard of quality, by agreeing to raise its research aspirations in return for a larger share of overhead costs.

Co-optation. A strategy of co-optation invites members of other stakeholder groups into the actual decision-making process. Colleges and universities have long co-opted the community by having citizen boards oversee their operations. At a much smaller level, a department might co-opt employers or alumni by establishing an advisory committee and giving it at least some authority (window dressing here doesn't count).

Coalition. Finally, a strategy of coalition occurs when one stakeholder group joins forces with another for the purpose of reaching a common goal. In higher education, coalitions are critical to the way the university functions, as Baldridge (1971) pointed out long ago; further, they tend to be temporary and ad hoc. Note, however, that a true coalition means the abandonment of autonomy vis a vis the other interest group in the embrace of a joint purpose. A department might seek out a coalition with other departments to counter a dean's desire to embark on a plan to reduce each department's hiring and spending authority.

So which of these strategies to choose? The Machiavellian response is to do whatever gains the department the most and costs it the least, taking into account the consequences of failure. This may seem cold-blooded, and in some ways it is, but consider two points. First, what has been outlined above is what Cervero and Wilson (1994) have characterized as a "substantively democratic process"; that is, it's a way for the department to pay explicit attention to its stakeholders without having the whole thing degenerate into a "disempowering relativism" (p. 140). Second, keep in mind that one of the cornerstones of academic professionalism is autonomy—pursuing knowledge and risking failure, unfettered by external political interests. In return for their autonomy, academic professionals consider their career a calling in the service of the public good. Otherwise they'd be little more than well-educated consultants. As I pointed out in an earlier chapter, academic faculty are not supposed to cater to every stakeholder's whim. They are, however, expected to serve the public good in ways informed by the public interest.

Negotiate the Department's Quality Standards, Starting With the Center and Working Outward

Stakeholders at or near the center will have the strongest voice and these interests must be negotiated carefully. As the department moves each successive step from inner to outer circles a "harder line" may be in order, with more competitive (read "persuasive" and "educative") strategies chosen and substantive changes made only when the consequences of not doing so are serious. (An obvious example here would be compliance with regional or specialized accreditation standards.)

I should point out that these steps are not linear. As departmental standards evolve, they should be placed before the faculty for review. These are, after all, their standards, those for which they are willing to be held mutually accountable. The process therefore is circular, or perhaps more precisely, spiral. Standards are never frozen, but fluid and evolving, changing as the interests of stakeholders change.

CONCLUSION

Does this mean that standard-setting never ends, that departments should be engaged in a never-ending cycle of developing quality standards and sounding out stakeholders? I can imagine eyes rolling as the reader contemplates this. As if departments and their chairs didn't already have too much to do! I sympathize, and I am not suggesting that what I have proposed above be done every year, or even every five years. I'd suggest, rather, that the entire process be done from scratch every ten years, timed to coincide perhaps with high-stakes exercises like accreditation and program review. Negotiated standards would then serve as points of departure for annual departmental and faculty workplans, and as negotiation levers (i.e., for discretionary resources) with central administration. Then perhaps every three-to-five years, depending on the degree of change in the institution, departmental standards might be revisited and fine-tuned by the faculty.

One final point. The values held by departmental faculty should not only be identified; they should also be examined and perhaps challenged as well. Walvoord and her colleagues (2000) reviewed the research literature on academic values and identified the following as most prominent: collegiality, autonomy, academic freedom, specialization/expertise, and reason and the scientific method. The authors suggest that not only might these values often conflict, they may also be incomplete: "the literature... may be ignoring some core values, especially... the value of service and of mentoring" (p. 17). The values most likely to be ignored by the faculty are precisely those most likely to surface when negotiating with the department's beneficiaries.

How is a department to know if its values are being served? By identifying and collecting appropriate evaluation evidence, the subject of the next chapter.

REFERENCES

Baldridge, J. V. (1971). *Power and conflict in the university: Research in the sociology of complex organizations.* New York, NY: Wiley.

Boyer, E. (1990). *Scholarship reconsidered: Priorities of the professoriate.* Princeton, NJ: Carnegie Foundation for the Advancement of Teaching.

Cervero, R. M., & Wilson, A. L. (1994). *Planning responsibly for adult education: A guide to negotiating power and interests.* San Francisco, CA: Jossey-Bass.

Gaff, J. G., Pruitt-Logan, A. S., Weibl, R. A., & Associates. (2000). *Building the faculty we need: Colleges and universities working together.* Washington, DC: Association of American Colleges and Universities.

Guba, E. G., & Lincoln, Y. S. (1989). *Fourth generation evaluation.* Newbury Park, CA: Sage.

McMillin, L. A., & Berberet, J. (Eds.). (2002). *A new academic compact: Revisioning the relationship between faculty and their institutions.* Bolton, MA: Anker.

Trower, C., Austin, A., & Sorcinelli, M. (2001, May). Paradise lost: How the academy converts enthusiastic recruits into early-career doubters. *AAHE Bulletin, 53* (9), 3-6.

Walvoord, B. E., Carey, A. K., Smith, H. L., Soled, S. W., Way, P. K., & Zorn, D. (2000). *Academic departments: How they work, how they change.* ASHE-ERIC Higher Education Report, 27 (8). San Francisco, CA: Jossey-Bass.

Wergin, J. F. (1976). Evaluation of organizational policymaking: A political model. *Review of Educational Research, 46* (1), 75-115.

FINDING EVIDENCE OF QUALITY
AND QUALITY EVIDENCE

6

The art of being wise is the art of

knowing what to overlook.

—William James

INTRODUCTION

True story: A flagship land-grant university in the Southeast, anxious to demonstrate its seriousness about public accountability, developed a comprehensive list of criteria for the review of academic departments. The factbook got a lot of press, including a glowing feature story in *The Chronicle of Higher Education.* The premise of the factbook was simple: Isolate indicators common to academic departments and their sister departments in peer institutions, and use these to determine where the university's departments ranked compared to their peers. I obtained a copy of the factbook and took a look at the specific criteria to be used to judge the various dimensions of quality. I was particularly curious about the criteria to be used to judge instructional quality. Three criteria were listed: 1) number of full-time faculty (graduate and undergraduate); 2) ratio of full-time faculty to undergraduate, master's, and doctoral students; and 3) degrees (baccalaureate, master's, and doctoral) awarded per faculty. That was it. Since more direct evidence of instructional quality was unavailable, at least in a form that was comparable across institutions, the powers-that-be at this university apparently felt that posting *some* data would show a good-faith effort, and would be preferable to showing nothing at all. But let's suppose that the psychology department at this university ranked eighth of ten peer institutions on the dimension of instructional effectiveness. What should it do to move up? The answer is clear: Lobby for more full-time faculty, recruit more students, and work on ways to keep them in the program longer. Setting aside for a moment the individual merits of these strategies, two obvious questions arise: What on earth do these criteria have to do with anyone's sense of what constitutes effective instruction? And what are the consequences to an institution and the students it serves if an academic department does what it feels is necessary to become more effective in this way? In other words, what are the consequential validity implications with this kind of goal displacement?

This story is, unfortunately, not an isolated example, just a particularly egregious one. In an attempt to become more accountable and to mollify its critics, Western higher education has embarked upon a highly dangerous course of chasing measures of quality that may have little to do with quality itself. I've already noted how this plays out as second- and third-tier institutions as defined by *U.S. News & World Report* seek to improve their status by becoming more selective and burnishing their research credentials, even when these actions run counter to institutional mission. Note, for example, how few comprehensive and urban universities appear in the *U.S. News'* first tier. Is it because these institutions don't provide students with an education to match the quality of a research university or a selective liberal arts college? Or is it because they are doing what they are supposed to be doing: focusing on developing the talent of that large group of students who may not possess stellar academic credentials but nevertheless have potential? Or providing a means for adult, nontraditional students to improve their lives by going to college part-time? What will happen as these institutions seek to emulate their more traditionally prestigious and well-endowed first-tier counterparts? Wouldn't we all be better off if institutions and their academic programs focused instead on how they contributed to the public good, acknowledging that different institutions do this in different ways? If academic programs are not to let their responsibility for defining appropriate evidence of academic quality default to system administrators and weekly newsmagazines, then how are they to do it themselves?

One of the many paradoxes in higher education has to do with our use of data. Here we are, a community devoted to the "search for truth and its free exposition" (AAUP, 1940); and yet we seem to use data mostly for the purposes of furthering political agendas. In the words of the Knight Higher Education Collaborative:

> *All too seldom do institutions make data the instruments of strategy in the fullest sense—to gauge the capacity of an institution to fulfill current commitments or pursue new opportunities, to understand external markets and the competition for new or existing programs and services, to analyze the opportunities for new ventures through collaboration among departments and centers, or to explore the prospect of even broader collaboration with other colleges and universities. While higher education exhibits a preoccupation with numbers like never before, institutions find themselves oddly stretched to both extremes of a spectrum expressed by these two [contradictory statements]: "We deferred any decision for want of sufficient data." And on the other, "We made the decision, data be damned." The ironic result is an institution that uses data extraordinarily well when rendering scholarly judgment but too often fails to use data effectively to improve its own operations, processes, and prospects. (2000, pp. 1-2)*

In this chapter I'll explore how academic programs might go about identifying and collecting data as true "instruments of strategy," as the Knight Collaborative puts it.

ASKING THE RIGHT QUESTIONS

In evaluating quality, the question is everything. All too often, program assessment begins with a discussion of which instruments to use, or perhaps what the program's goals are. Neither is a particularly useful place to begin. If the evaluation is to be one that is truly meaningful to those affected by it, it has to begin with the questions these people have. And make no mistake: Faculty members have plenty of questions about the quality of their work, both individually and collectively, and these will be stimulated particularly when the department has gone through a values-negotiating process such as the one suggested in the previous chapter. A simple and useful exercise is to ask department members stimulus questions like these: "What do you want to know that will help our department make better choices about how to use our resources? What information might help us enhance the quality of the work we do?" (Ferren & Slavings, 2000). The key is in acknowledging these questions, negotiating them among departmental faculty, and framing them in ways that lead to the identification of useful evidence. Michael Quinn Patton, a longtime proponent of what he calls "utilization-focused evaluation" (1997), suggests five criteria for good evaluation questions:

1) Data can be brought to bear on the question; that is, it is a truly empirical question.

2) There is more than one possible answer to the question; that is, the answer is not predetermined by the phrasing of the question.

3) The primary intended users want information to help answer the question. They care about the answer.

4) The primary users want to answer the question for themselves, not just for someone else.

5) The intended users can indicate how they would use the answer to the question; that is, they can specify the relevance of an answer to the question for future action. (p. 32)

Some Bad Evaluation Questions

Here are some examples of bad evaluation questions, and ways they could be improved:

How do we convince the administration that we need more faculty lines? This isn't an empirical question; it's a political question.

Are we doing a good job teaching undergraduates? While this question may be a place to start, it's so broad and vague as to be almost unanswerable in its present form. A better place to begin is with what the department expects its students to learn, then to assess its success in producing that learning. A question phrased in this way will almost invariably raise further and deeper questions about curricular relevance, currency, and coherence.

How can we document learning outcomes for our accreditation self study? This isn't an evaluation question; it's an instrumental question. It's a question about how to collect data that someone else wants.

What can we do about senior faculty deadwood? While this is a question that has come up in countless private conversations among faculty (all of them non-deadwood, of course), it's loaded with presuppositions about what constitutes deadwood. Further, the very connotations of the term suggest that there's only one satisfactory answer, and that is to find a way to ease out the lifeless faculty in favor of new blood. Looking at these faculty members differently, as "driftwood" perhaps, might lead to a different kind of question: "What viable options exist to help revitalize senior faculty?"

How can we get the school's promotion and tenure committee to reward teaching on a par with research? Again, a political, not an empirical, question. It presumes that the evaluation question ("Does the Promotion and Tenure Committee reward faculty work in ways that are consistent with guidelines?") has already been answered.

Why are students only interested in getting good jobs? Again, there's a presumption of fact here that begs for challenge. A better evaluation question would be, "What are the principal expectations our majors have of us, and how well are we meeting them?" If it turns out that student expectations are not in sync with what the faculty think they should be, then the question becomes one of how to negotiate values, in ways suggested in Chapter 5.

Some Good Evaluation Questions

Here, on the other hand, are some good evaluation questions, good in the sense that they meet criteria 1, 2, 4, and 5 listed above. These are just sample questions; the list is neither comprehensive nor exhaustive. Whether they meet criterion 3, however—that is, whether they're appropriate for your department—is for your department to decide. These are just sample questions; the list is intended to be neither comprehensive nor exhaustive.

Student learning. How well do course objectives track with curricular objectives? How consistent is student learning across multiple sections of the same course? To what extent are key curricular goals introduced and reinforced appropriately from course to course? Do student course-taking patterns reflect the most appropriate sequences? Are students suitably prepared for graduate school and/or chosen careers?

Student success. What factors cause students to switch to another major? What is most responsible for success or failure of at-risk students? What is our track record in attracting and retaining students of color? How confident are students in their ability to compete in the marketplace? How well do graduates accomplish their career goals?

Curricular efficiency. How well do our service courses contribute to the institution's general education goals? To what extent are curricular objectives based on documented evidence of what students need to know and do? What is the trend in student credit hours at graduation, and is this number excessive? How many course sections are under-enrolled, and is this number excessive? How many discretionary courses are offered, and is this number excessive?

Scholarly productivity. What are the research trajectories of department faculty? Do these converge in ways consistent with departmental and institutional research priorities? How well is the department gaining access to information about grants available to support faculty scholarship? What investments in the research infrastructure might make departmental faculty more competitive in landing research awards? To what degree is faculty scholarship finding appropriate outlets?

Resource management. What is the impact of courses taught by part-time or adjunct faculty on student learning and curricular coherence? What is the appropriate trade-off between class size and student engagement? Between the number of distance-learning sections and student engagement? Has the department made appropriate use of discretionary income (e.g., overhead generated by research grants)?

Departmental engagement. How much do departmental faculty know about the work their colleagues do? What are the most appropriate ways for faculty to initiate and sustain collaborative endeavors in their teaching and scholarship? To what degree do the faculty share a sense of the collective work of the department and a sense of collective responsibility for its work? To what extent are departmental issues subject to open and constructive debate? How does the department add value to the school or institution, and to the community?

IDENTIFYING POTENTIALLY USEFUL EVIDENCE

A common, but erroneous, assumption is that evidence and data are synonymous terms. They are not. Linking them has lead to the dubious practice of collecting any and all kinds of information that might be relevant to the question at hand, and presenting these data en masse, expecting that somehow an invisible hand will help the reader sort through it all and find the truth. Consider, for example, the volumes of data collected for institutional self studies, or as part of various strategic planning initiatives. But how much of this information is deliberately organized to support a claim or to help reconcile competing claims? In other words, how much of this information is used as evidence? Peter Ewell (2002) has noted that evidence has five distinguishing characteristics:

Evidence Is Intentional and Purposive

Evidence is used to advance an argument. Just as in a courtroom, evidence is presented to make a case. A college's fact book is not, by itself, evidence, while a profile of entering students, compiled to show how student characteristics have changed over time, is. Evidence is always contextual to the argument being made.

Evidence Becomes Evidence Only as a Result of Interpretation and Reflection

As Ewell notes, evidence does not speak for itself, but rather implies that there has been an attempt to make meaning of the data—to show how the evidence leads to a better understanding of an issue or phenomenon.

Evidence Is Integrated and Holistic

Individual bits of data take on meaning only within the context of the larger case. Thus, one speaks of the body of evidence, or the weight of the evidence. The evidence for quality in an academic department may take many forms, but all of these need to hang together to support the claim being made.

Evidence Can Be Both Quantitative and Qualitative

Neither type of evidence is inherently superior to the other: It all depends upon how evidence is being used. Numbers can be quite useful to cut through specious thinking and fuzzy rhetoric; text can be most useful to tell the story of a program and to help readers draw connections to their own situations.

Evidence May Be Either Direct or Indirect

Sometimes it's neither feasible nor desirable to measure a quality directly; surrogate or proxy measures are more effective. For example, one might consider a comprehensive examination to be the most direct source of evidence of student learning in the major, but because of its narrow focus, other more indirect measures, such as student focus groups and acceptance rates into graduate school, may be needed to round out the portrayal.

In short, then, data are transformed into evidence by means of human interpretation. Thus, determining what constitutes evidence—or, more important, what the data might be evidence of—is a highly judgmental process. That's why the same set of data can often be used to drive contrary arguments. For example, do high GRE scores earned by a department's graduates constitute evidence of a department's success in educating majors? Or do they show departmental bias toward preparing students for graduate school, at the expense of other career options? Or, if the institution is highly selective in the first place, do they show not much of anything at all, other than the high predictability of academic ability upon admission? The point is that, just as data don't speak for themselves, evidence doesn't either. What good evidence does, or should do, is to engage department members and others in a useful, more informed dialogue about what's going on. In these dialogues one can expect multiple truths to emerge, and if this in turn leads to constructive contention, that's a good thing.

The Pew study of departmental assessment (Wergin & Swingen, 2000) uncovered a wide array of evidence used to assess departmental quality, as Table 6.1 indicates.

TABLE 6.1

EVIDENCE USED FOR DEPARTMENTAL ASSESSMENT

Faculty qualifications	Academic origins/credentials
	National prominence
	Qualifications of adjuncts
	Potential for response to future needs/opportunities
	Congruence of faculty qualifications with departmental needs/goals
	Faculty development opportunities
Faculty productivity	Research funding
	Faculty publications
	Scholarly awards

	National standing of department
	Teaching loads
	Student credit hours (SCH) taught
	Dispersion of faculty FTE
	Theses advised, chaired
	Students supervised
	Service contributions
	Academic outreach
	Collaboration with other units or programs
Efficiency	Trends in unit costs
	Faculty/student FTE
	Faculty/staff FTE
	SCH/faculty FTE
	Revenues/SCH
	Revenues/costs
	Operating budget/faculty FTE
	Research expenditures/faculty FTE
	State support/total budget
Curricular quality	Planning processes
	Quality control mechanisms
	Learning goals
	Requirements for major or graduate degree
	Congruence of course/curricular goals
	Course coordination
	Prerequisite patterns
	Balance between depth and breadth
	Percentage of courses involving active learning
	Uniformity across multiple course sections
	Availability of electives
	Advising procedures

	Role in general education/service courses
	Use of adjunct faculty
	Use of student portfolios, competency exams, capstone courses
	Curricular revision procedures
Pedagogical quality	Processes for evaluation of teaching and advising
	Engagement in collaborative teaching
	Class size
	Pedagogical innovation
	Characteristics of course syllabi
	Strategies for promoting active learning
	Procedures for setting academic standards
	Adoption of information technology
Student quality	Entering SAT, ACT, or GRE scores
	Recruitment strategies
	Acceptance ratio
	Monetary support for graduate students
	Demographic diversity
Student productivity	Enrollment patterns
	Number of majors
	Number of transfers in
	Demands on students
	Student effort
	Retention/graduation rates
	Degrees awarded
	Time to degree
	Student involvement in departmental activities
Learning outcomes	Processes for evaluating learning
	Student cognitive development
	Student satisfaction
	Grade distributions

	Mastery of generic skills
	Student achievements
	Accomplishment of objectives in major
	Performance in capstone courses
	Student placement
	Employer satisfaction
	Alumni satisfaction
	Performance on licensing/certification exams, standardized tests
	Percentage of graduates entering graduate school
Adequacy of resources	Laboratory/computer facilities
	Faculty offices
	Classrooms
	Support staff, number and qualifications
	Enrollment capacity
Contributions to institutional mission/priorities	Departmental mission/vision
	Departmental distinctiveness
	Centrality to institution
	Availability of program elsewhere
	Relationship to other programs
	Contribution to economic development, other social benefits
	Service to non-majors, continuing education
	Fit with strategic plan
	Student demand
	Employer demand

(Adapted from J. F. Wergin and J. N. Swingen, Departmental Assessment, 2000)

More than 100 separate criteria are represented here. Contrary to conventional wisdom, even a cursory examination of this table indicates a fairly even distribution across input (faculty qualifications, FTEs), process (curricular quality, demands on students), and output (faculty publications, student learning) criteria. Looking more closely at the process criteria, however, reveals that relatively few relate to how well a department or program promotes faculty and student learning, development, and growth. If continuous improvement is a valued goal, it doesn't appear to be evaluated (and thus rewarded) very often. Still, this table represents, at the very least, a great deal of potentially useful data. No institution does, or should, collect all of these data, although we found that most institutions did have most of these sources of evidence available to them. The question then becomes how to take raw, uninterpreted information and transform it into useful evidence?

JUDGING THE QUALITY OF EVIDENCE

Despite the fact that virtually no policies on institutional program review contain guidelines for judging the validity of the evidence to be used, guidelines for quality do exist. As I've suggested already, the answer to any question of validity depends on the extent to which the evidence fits the context: Assessing student quality by computing acceptance ratios will be far more appropriate for a selective national university than for a regional comprehensive. With that in mind it should be possible for institutions and their departments to examine carefully the evidence they use to assist with judgments about program quality. A framework for this is already available, in the form of *Program Evaluation Standards* (2nd Ed.) (Joint Committee, 1994). While these standards were written generically to cover all forms of educational evaluation, most of them apply equally well to the evaluation of higher education programs. The standards are organized into four categories. Paraphrased, these are

1) **Utility standards:** intended to ensure that evaluation data will serve the needs of the program's stakeholders

2) **Feasibility standards:** intended to ensure that an evaluation will be realistic, prudent, diplomatic, and frugal

3) **Propriety standards:** intended to ensure that the evaluation will be undertaken legally, ethically, and with due regard for those affected by its results

4) Accuracy standards: intended to ensure that the evaluation will convey technically accurate information about the program

Accuracy standards are those which address questions of data validity. One of the accuracy standards, paraphrased, says this: Information-gathering procedures should be developed in ways that will assure that interpretations of data will be valid for the intended use. Criteria and evidence are not inherently valid or invalid; rather validity "depends specifically on the questions being addressed, the procedure used, the conditions of data collection, ... and especially the interpretation of the results" (1994, p. 146). Ewell (2002) posits five principles of good evidence, similar to those promulgated by the Joint Committee:

1) Relevant: Evidence is "demonstrably related to the claim being made... Including what any information advanced is supposed to be evidence of" (pp. 8-9).

2) Verifiable: Sufficient information is available to allow for independent corroboration by others.

3) Representative: Evidence is "typical of an underlying situation or condition and not an isolated case" (p. 11).

4) Cumulative: Credibility of evidence is enhanced with the use of multiple sources.

5) Actionable: Evidence provides "specific guidance for action and improvement... The evidence provided [should be] reflectively analyzed and interpreted to reveal its specific implications" (p.13).

Guidelines for Judging the Quality of Evidence

Combining these two sources of wisdom about assessing the evidentiary quality of data suggests the following guidelines.

1) Look for congruence between potential evidence and the program's values and goals. Obtain judgments from the program's stakeholders (faculty, administrators, students) about the evidence's credibility.

2) Specify reasons for selecting data to be used as evidence, and show the link between the evidence and the questions and issues being addressed. Avoid selecting information just because it is quantifiable or readily available.

3) Be especially careful when adopting new instruments or instruments originally developed for another purpose. Do not rule them out, but point out that these instruments are exploratory and must be interpreted with caution and within strictly defined contextual limits.

4) Compile evidence using multiple sources of data, but do so in as nondisruptive and parsimonious a manner as possible.

5) Assess the comprehensiveness of the evidence as a set, relative to the information needed to answer the set of evaluation questions. Ask, "Will all this information together tell us what we need to know?"

6) Prepare to answer a series of "what if" questions: "What will we do if the evidence shows...?"

Judging the Quality of Evidence: An Example

Here is an example of how a department might go about identifying appropriate evidence for its evaluation questions.

The phrenology department has for some years identified civic engagement as one of its top priorities, in keeping with its role as a major department in an urban comprehensive university. This has taken the form of service-learning courses, which now occupy 20% of the curriculum, professional service projects, and shared research with community agencies. While there is plenty of anecdotal evidence that the engagement strategy is working, questions remain about whether it's worth all the effort. Junior faculty are especially concerned that their commitment to engagement will hurt them at promotion and tenure time, when they may have less traditional evidence of merit (such as refereed publications) in their portfolios. The central evaluation question before the department, therefore, is, "How do we know we are effective in our community partnerships?" A first round of discussion leads to agreement that the following kinds of evidence demonstrate effectiveness (or lack of effectiveness) (Gelmon, 1997):

- Student satisfaction with partnerships
- Community satisfaction with partnerships
- Connections of community-based scholarship to scholarly agendas and resultant publications, presentations, and grants
- Changes in policy or professional practice traceable to partnership activities

When faculty are asked, "Will this information together tell us what we need to know?," it becomes clear that effectiveness will be hard to demonstrate without the following added to the list:

- Student learning outcomes consistent with curricular goals

When department faculty consider what they will be able to do with the evidence collected, they realize that having the above data alone would provide little guidance on what to maintain, enhance, or change, and so the following is added to the list:

- The nature of the partnerships negotiated between the department and its community partners, including the patterns of involvement, kinds of activities conducted, and source and methods of initiation of contact

The department then considers what form the evidence should take. Data on scholarly products are already available and need only to be pulled together and profiled. Data on student satisfaction and learning are already available in part from end-of-course surveys and course projects, although upon inspection it is quickly apparent that they are insufficient as evidence, and so the department decides to ask students to prepare reflective essays on their experiences in service-learning courses. The origin of the partnerships and patterns of involvement, as well as the level of satisfaction of community partners and the impact of the department's work with them, is to be determined by a brief survey and a few selected interviews (see Palomba & Banta, 1999) augmented by document review.

So the department compiles its evidence. Now what? In the next chapter, I discuss how to make meaning of what the department has learned.

REFERENCES

American Association of University Professors. (1940, 1995). *AAUP policy documents and reports.* Washington, DC: author.

Ewell, P. (2002). *Evidence guide: A guide to using evidence in the accreditation process.* Alameda, CA: Western Association of Schools and Colleges.

Ferren, A. S., & Slavings, R. (2000). *Investing in quality: Tools for improving curricular efficiency.* Washington, DC: Association of American Colleges and Universities.

Gelmon, S. B. (1997). *Intentional improvement: The deliberate linkage of assessment and accreditation.* Presentation to the 1997 AAHE Conference on Assessment and Quality. Washington, DC: American Association for Higher Education.

Joint Committee on Standards for Educational Evaluation, James R. Sanders, chair. (1994). *The program evaluation standards: How to assess evaluations of educational programs.* Thousand Oaks, CA: Sage.

Palomba, C. A., & Banta, T. W. (1999). *Assessment essentials: Planning, implementing, and improving assessment in higher education.* San Francisco, CA: Jossey-Bass.

Patton, M. Q. (1997). *Utilization-focused evaluation: The new century text.* Thousand Oaks, CA: Sage.

Wergin, J. F., & Swingen, J. N. (2000). *Departmental assessment: How some colleges are effectively evaluating the collective work of faculty.* Washington, DC: AAHE.

MAKING MEANING OF QUALITY EVIDENCE

We are wiser than we know.

—Ralph Waldo Emerson

The most dangerous thing in the world is to think
you understand something.

—Zen saying

INTRODUCTION

As I've suggested in previous chapters, the search for program quality is ultimately a highly personal and interpretive act. Quality is never defined by numbers and statistics, or by stories and testimonials. The act of judging value occurs as individual people take in information, make meaning of it by filtering it through their own cognitive perspectives and value orientations, and then render a judgment, a judgment which is often tacit and not even conscious.

In this chapter, I focus on how a department might interpret and use the information it collects about itself and how it might do so in a way which leads to a more critically reflective culture. I'll address these questions: How do we interpret the evaluative evidence we've collected, and how do we do this within the context of an academic collective? How do we use this evidence to challenge the assumptions we make about what we're doing and the effects we're having on our stakeholders? How do we use data to inform better decision-making?

All too often, it seems, we assume that judgments of quality will become obvious once we look at the evidence, and we assume that the standards we use to make these judgments will be absolute and held by all. Neither of these assumptions is true. Let's return to the four statements I used to begin Chapter 5:

> *Enrollment trends in our major are down, and we need to do something about it.*

> *Students are complaining about the senior seminar being too hard. How did we get such a bunch of crybabies?*

> *We've had a productive year—a record number of single-authored publications in refereed journals.*

> *Our graduate students seem content to land academic jobs in second- and third-tier institutions. Where have we failed?*

Notice that in each of these statements clear value judgments are made, based on implicit standards of performance. These judgments then lead to conclusions about what the department should do. Negotiating departmental values in the manner suggested in Chapter 5 will make the assumptions behind these conclusions clearer, but they won't necessarily resolve debate. The department may already have negotiated the value of having a strong enrollment, and it may even have imagined what the ideal enrollment should be; but does that mean that any drop in enrollment is a sign of trouble? How loud and vociferous do student complaints have to be before some collective action is warranted? Could a productive year in scholarship be indicated in other ways? How many graduates would have to be placed in first-tier institutions in order for the faculty to feel successful as mentors?

STANDARDS: A DEFINITION

In this chapter, I lay out a strategy for determining standards of quality for a program and for making meaning of the quality evidence presented to it. First, however, I want to clarify the term "standard" itself. Like "quality," "standard" is a fuzzy concept. While the term "criteria" refers to the kinds of evidence used to inform judgments of value, a "standard" is a point of comparison for a particular criterion, and thus provides a basis for a judgment of value. If you imagine criteria as metaphorical yardsticks, then standards are the markers on the stick. For example, one departmental criterion might be "majors who complete their course of study within six years." This information isn't of much use by itself. What's considered acceptable performance? 60%? 70%? 80%? Higher than last year? At the 50th percentile of peer institutions? A standard, therefore, is a level of performance against which evaluative evidence might be compared and judgments about value drawn. There are several ways of framing standards:

Standards as Goals

We're all familiar with setting goals. We set performance goals, annually or for some other time interval. Faculty members set them with their chairs, departments set them with their deans, schools set them with the central administration, and institutions set them with their boards. Actual performance is compared to intended performance and a judgment is made. If only the world were that simple! The limitations of goals as standards are serious. Consider this: "Sally, your annual workplan indicated that you would publish three articles and a book chapter this year. I see here that you've published two articles, but the third article is only in press and the book chapter is still under review. I'll have to give you a rating of 'less than satisfactory' in scholarship." As useful as performance goals may be as tools for organizing thinking and focusing on results, they pose serious problems for making judgments of value.

They assume perfect information and total predictability. It's one thing to talk about our aspirations, or what we dream of becoming—

in fact, Senge (2000) suggests that group aspirations are key to organizational learning—but it's quite another to pin these down into concrete objectives for which we reasonably might be held accountable. A host of unexpected problems or opportunities can arise, even in the relatively stable rhythm of academic life, and these can make the clearest and most well thought-out goals less important, if not downright irrelevant. Further, because the future is so hazy and unpredictable, numbers are often just pulled out of the air in an attempt to make the goals look more precise. How attainable is an 80% retention rate in five years? No one really knows.

They pose conflicts of interest. Evaluator Michael Quinn Patton (1997) reports seeing the following poster on an office wall: "The greatest danger is not that we aim too high and miss, but that our goal is too low and we attain it" (p. 154). In other words, setting low expectations is good if you want to appear successful, but bad if you want to achieve real quality. Goal-setters are confronted with this dilemma all the time.

An obsession with measurable goals can take the life out of a program and deflect it from its real purposes. I've addressed this point before as the phenomenon of "goal displacement" (Blau & Scott, 1962). It's one thing to consider certain quantitative indicators such as admission and retention rates, grant dollars generated, and so on, as evidence of program quality, but it's quite another to fix on these indicators as goals themselves. For example, if a department sets a goal for itself that it will increase its enrollment of majors by 30% over the next five years, that's fine, as long as everyone is clear that simply accomplishing that goal doesn't necessarily improve program quality (or, conversely, that failing to achieve that goal doesn't necessarily indicate failure). Faculty must ask themselves this question over and over again: "What will be the consequences of accomplishing this goal? How will that contribute to our core purposes?"

Again, I don't mean to imply that having departments set collective goals is a bad idea. Quite the contrary. Program goals reflect, in a results-oriented, forward-looking way, what the department stands for and what it intends to accomplish. Goals as performance targets are good. Problems arise only when goals shift from being used, not as tools to focus energy and commitment, but as standards by which the program is to be held accountable.

Standards as History

A department can compare its performance to outcomes of previous years or collections of years. The longer the trendline, the better, to help distinguish real trends from temporary aberrations. Obvious candidates for this kind of analysis include enrollment and retention data, course and faculty FTEs, extramural grant dollars, and so forth. Looking at current performance as part of a long-term trend has the additional advantage of acknowledging change by accretion, which may not be noticeable in the short run. Zemsky and Massy (1993), for example, have written about the phenomenon of the academic ratchet, in which reductions in teaching load for high-profile research faculty then become the standard teaching load for everyone. Departments where the ratchet operates probably don't even realize it—until they see the trend lines, that is. The problem with history as a standard is, of course, history itself. Looking backward doesn't always help a department look forward.

Standards as Tacit Judgments

This approach to standards comes from a different perspective altogether. It assumes that such complex qualities as educational programs are not easily amenable to analytic approaches that result in specific outcome statements, but rather that the ingredients of a quality program are far more ineffable than that. Value judgments, therefore, should be made on the basis of a more holistic assessment, undertaken by academics who are thoroughly steeped in the purposes and traditions of the academy. Such a perspective is what undergirds the use of high-profile colleagues in other institutions as peer reviewers: While they may be given a great deal of information about program purposes and goals, their main concern is in looking at the program as a whole and delivering an assessment of it from their position as expert. There's a lot to be said for this approach: Obtaining an external perspective on the value of the program, filtered through the lens of a connoisseur (Eisner, 1991), can be hugely valuable as a way of challenging assumptions and getting departments and their faculty to see themselves differently. As Eisner points out, "We need to learn to see what we have learned not to notice" (p. 77). But there are some obvious drawbacks, as well. Chief among these is that standards are never explicit, by definition. They depend entirely upon the expert making the judgment. And so while the tacit judgments of outside experts might be useful and powerful as a source of judgments on program quality, they make sense only as an adjunct technique.

Standards as Benchmarks

"Benchmarking" has become another one of those terms imported from the quality movement in the business world and as such has carried with it the usual baggage. In its broadest sense, benchmarking simply refers to the practice of identifying institutions or departments similar to your own who engage in best practices (however defined), and using these practices as standards for comparison. Outcomes of other institutions can be very useful as a source of aspiration, especially for those who might otherwise be cynical or pessimistic about the institution's own potential. Faculty in an arts and science department in a large research university might assume that learning communities consisting of small intact student cohorts are simply not possible in an institution like theirs until they hear about how it has worked in an institution to which they would like to be compared. At that point what Lee Shulman calls "diffusion by envy" (1995) takes over. An overreliance on standards as benchmarks has clear liabilities, however. Peer institutions, no matter how similar they appear, are different in innumerable and important ways—structurally, culturally, financially, and historically, not to mention differences in personalities and leadership styles. Outcomes that fit Susquehanna may simply be unrealistic for Quinippiac, and vice-versa.

Standards Defined by Discipline, Profession, or Accreditation Guidelines

Programs ignore national standards set by external bodies at their peril, and so few do. It's also difficult to imagine any department being satisfied, however, with simply meeting the minimum standards set by these agencies.

Your department isn't limited to only one of these comparisons, of course, because each has unique strengths and weaknesses, combinations are not only possible but desirable. Evidence concerning enrollment is most likely to be meaningful when compared to past years; evidence concerning curricular process is most likely to be meaningful when compared to similar or exemplary programs; evidence of student performance may well use all of the above. What's important is to be clear up front about what the points of comparison will be and to gain the consensus of department members.

If your department is at all typical, data flow into it all the time: enrollment and retention statistics, demographic profiles, credit hours generated, and so on. Add to this the results of graduate and employer surveys, student focus groups, market surveys, and other ad hoc measures, and any point of view will probably find some datum useful to support it. If not, well, then one could argue that the department isn't getting the right data or the data it's getting are fatally flawed. Occasionally on a slow Saturday night I'll watch "The Capital Gang" on CNN; I always get a kick out of how Robert Novak, the conservative commentator, will use virtually any piece of data about the national economy to argue how it supports the need for a cut in the capital gains tax. (Liberal pundits do the same thing, of course, with their own pet ideas.) It's only when the evidence is overwhelming, it seems, that people are willing to reconsider their views.

It doesn't have to be this way. Other scenarios are possible. What's required is a different way of thinking about data, and a different way of thinking about human learning. Recall the discussion in Chapter 4 about learning as transformation. The key to making evaluative evidence useful is to create a set of conditions under which faculty are most likely to pay attention to it, and that occurs when the evidence is presented in a way that creates a "disorienting dilemma," in Mezirow's terms (1990): It's not obvious or easily explained, and it doesn't simply reinforce existing values or prejudices. (If the evidence is truly overwhelming, such as finding out that large numbers of students are suddenly failing board exams, it may also be necessary to deal with faculty anxiety before any rational discussion is possible.)

Recall from Chapter 4 the characteristics most fertile for critical inquiry in a department: asking open-ended questions, reflecting about what it does, sharing individual reflections through discourse, making meaning of data, and connecting reflection with action. I'll spend the rest of this chapter taking up these last two points.

INTERPRETING EVALUATIVE DATA

Engaging in useful discussions about the meaning of data requires a strategy for focusing these discussions. Patton, in *Utilization-Focused Evaluation* (1997), provides some useful ideas, and I will be drawing freely from his book. Useful interpretation of evaluative evidence has several steps.

Setting the Stage for Use

It's helpful right at the outset to ask a series of "what-if" questions about the data. Prior to reporting the evidence, invite department members to reflect on what various findings might mean to them. Ask, "What would indicate low quality, acceptable quality, and exemplary quality to you?" Present them with hypothetical data and ask, "What would you make of these data? What actions should we take if we got these results?"

These questions not only encourage reflective thinking before positions become solidified; they also help department members identify what might be most useful to them, and what important questions they may have neglected to ask. For example, suppose that the department were about to review the results of a focus group of recent graduates. Faculty members might say that low quality would be suggested if more than half of alumni felt inadequately prepared with respect to two or more curricular goals, exemplary quality would be suggested if 80% of alumni felt adequately prepared in all areas, and acceptable quality would be reflected by anything in between. Asking these stage-setting questions gets the collective faculty values on the table and forestalls potential defensiveness later on.

Present Data Simply

The principle of Ockam's Razor—that the simplest of two or more competing theories is preferable—applies here, the maxim that the simplest explanation is the one most likely to be true. Massive data tables with columns and columns of numbers are not likely to lead to much meaning-making. Neither are highly esoteric analysis procedures if they are not accompanied by simple displays. On the other hand, inviting department members to root around in raw data may lead to useful insights if the expectation is that their rooting will lead to a simpler display. As Patton (1997) notes, it's important to balance the complexity of real life with simplicity of presentation: Making the data understandable does not mean having to boil everything down to single percentages or ratios. Sometimes an appropriate balance will require the presentation of multiple perspectives. For example, suppose the department were looking at trends in the enrollment of ethnic minorities, having determined that a more diverse student body leads to a richer learning experience and thus a higher quality curriculum. Suppose the trends looked like those in Table 7.1.

TABLE 7.1

ENROLLMENT TRENDS: MINORITY/NON-MINORITY STUDENTS

	Five years ago	Today	Absolute change	%
Minorities	20	25	5	25
Non-minorities	100	120	20	20

Is the student body more diverse today, or not? The answer depends on whether the focus is on absolute or relative change.

One of the reasons why there has been such a trend toward the use of more qualitative data in evaluation (case studies, interviews, stories, and so forth) is because of the false precision given to numbers. We have all witnessed the horrors of some department chair calculating mean student ratings of faculty down to the second decimal point, then using the result to rank-order faculty for merit increases. The problem is not that numbers shouldn't be used; the problem is that the numbers are not interpreted appropriately. Presenting data simply does not mean succumbing to reductionistic fallacies. Such problems are avoided when the data are interpreted in ways suggested below.

Identify Claims and Concerns Emerging From the Data; Negotiate Issues of Interpretation

No matter how powerful or persuasive the evidence may be on its face, and no matter how well the department has been prepped for the evidence by identifying levels of desirability, interpretations and value judgments will inevitably rest with the interplay between the data, as stimuli, and the value perspectives of those reviewing the data. Evaluative evidence by itself doesn't answer questions but rather makes the questions sharper and more well-informed. Answers are value judgments and thus are highly personal.

Here's an example to help clarify the process. Suppose a department of urban planning were reviewing student learning outcomes in the major as evidence of quality in their undergraduate program. Department members had already decided to look at the capstone course as a principal source of evidence, specifically the extent to which seniors were able to integrate knowledge from previous courses in the major. Imagine a conversation like the following as faculty review student projects:

> *I like the way the students have applied general systems theory to urban problems. They seem to have grasped the idea that working on one problem is likely to affect another. (claim)*

Maybe so, but they don't seem to quite understand that change isn't linear. I would like to have seen more flexibility and built-in experimentation in their projects. (concern)

Oh, I think there's plenty of flexibility in these plans. Students are, after all, just learning the rules of the game here. The real flexibility will come later, when they're out on the job. (issue)

Claims are, in essence, value judgments indicating that standards have been met, while concerns are judgments that they have not been met. Once consensus is reached on claims and concerns, attention should turn to the issues, or points where interpretation has diverged. Recall from Chapter 5 that the first question to ask of issues is whether they are worth worrying about. More often than not the answer will be no, and so the appropriate course will be simply to agree to disagree. If, however, the answer is yes, and the issue is not one which can be resolved empirically, then the department has uncovered deeper fissures in values, and they need to be negotiated in ways described in Chapter 5.

CONNECTING REFLECTION WITH ACTION

This used to be called closing the loop, before closing the loop became yet another assessment cliché. Actually I never much liked the term anyway, because it implies tying up the process in a way that's all clean and neat. Still, critical reflection that does not lead to actionable consequences seems like a monumental waste of time to me, despite whatever deep learning may have been left in its wake. Connecting reflection to action suggests the following steps.

Take Stock

Doing something useful with new insights requires, first, that the department take stock. What does the evidence suggest about our collective strengths and weaknesses? Or to put it somewhat more crassly, how might we leverage our position for maximum competitive advantage? Does the evidence suggest that our mission has evolved, maybe in imperceptible ways? What appears to be our niche, in the school, institution, and discipline? How comfortable are we with that? How does what we have learned about ourselves affect who we are and what we aspire to become?

Revisit Claims and Concerns

Then the department can revisit its claims and concerns and see what they add up to. Do claims and concerns reflect the central values of the department? If the claims continue to hold, and the concerns are successfully addressed, will the department become what it aspires to become? If not, what's missing, and how might the gaps be redefined as opportunities?

Address the Program's Beneficiaries

The outcomes of these discussions can then be used to address the program's beneficiaries. It's useful at this point to return to the notion of adding value: Consider how the program adds value to its students, the school or institution, and the discipline or profession (claims), and how value could be enhanced by addressing certain key problems (concerns). Address local stakeholder groups and sound them out.

To students: "We meet your learning needs by... and we would like to enhance your learning by... How does this match your learning needs?"

To alumni: "Students gain the following from our curriculum... and we would like to enhance their learning by addressing the following concerns... How well does this match your sense of what our priorities should be?"

To central administration: "We add value to the institution in the following ways... and we propose to address the following, which should enhance our value... How does this match your sense of what our department's role should be?"

Develop an Action Plan

Use stakeholder feedback as raw material from which to fashion an action plan. Sounding out program beneficiaries about what the department has to offer them and where it comes up short does not require that the department become a toady to others' interests. On the contrary, because it has taken the initiative and set the agenda, the department positions itself more powerfully. As I noted in Chapter 5, having a clearer sense about how it is valued by its stakeholders enables the department to behave proactively by selecting negotiating strategies which best fit the power relationships, rather than acting without that knowledge, or worse, sitting back and doing nothing until the ax threatens to fall.

Creating an action plan can be a deadly—and in the long run, unproductive—process, as innumerable institutions have learned with various forms of strategic planning. Earlier in this book, I was critical of the practice of using goals as standards for quality, not because having goals is a bad thing, but rather because using goals as standards presumes a rational and predictable world. Unforseen events, opportunities, and problems can make even the most thoughtful of goals hopelessly obsolete.

So, then, why plan? Why not simply get along by "muddling through," to borrow Braybrooke and Lindblom's (1963) classic phrase? Tierney, in his wonderfully engaging book *Building the Responsive Campus* (1999), has the answer, I think. While he agrees that the militaristic images of strategic planning (rallying the troops to solve identified problems) leads to planning that is linear, myopic, and counterproductive, he also argues that colleges and universities suffer from a form of "institutional deficit disorder" (p. 75) by lurching from one change initiative to the next. They suffer, in other words, from a lack of strategic thinking. While it appears that Tierney may be giving contradictory advice here, he isn't. What he proposes is that institutions (and by implication, departments) develop visions of who they are and what they wish to become based on history, culture, experience, and a thorough knowledge of their constituencies. And then, rather than attacking the vision as if it were Pork Chop Hill, the wise organization will instead encourage creative thinking by supporting experimentation, trial and error, and opportunism. What's required of these efforts, however, is critical reflection: How is what we are doing congruent with and supportive of our vision? How are we and the institution and its students better off? How does what we have done contribute to a climate supportive of creative thinking and problem solving? This kind of thinking leads to what Ramaley (1998, personal communication) in another context has called the management of reasonable risk. Empirical support for Tierney's ideas may be found in the report of *The Futures Project* (Smith, 1998), a comprehensive study of change in 18 colleges and universities in California, where the greatest change occurred in institutions with cultures of experimentation, not those with high-profile strategic plans.

DEPARTMENT QUALITY: A DEFINITION

And so connecting reflection with action doesn't go just one way, and doesn't just close the loop. The best kind of action is that which itself leads to further reflection. We live in a chaotic and turbulent world, even in the academy. Quality departments and programs know this. They act on that knowledge by developing a collective vision that makes sense, given departmental resources and institutional context; by listening carefully to the interests of their stakeholders and responding to these in a way that is genuine but yet does not compromise their academic freedom and autonomy; by nurturing and supporting experimentation in a way that does not frown on failure but rather encourages learning; and by acting on what they learn about themselves in a way that faculty become more connected to their stakeholders and to each other. If I had to come up with a single definition of "departmental quality," that would be it.

REFERENCES

Blau, P. M., & Scott, W. R. (1962). *Formal organizations: A comparative approach.* San Francisco, CA: Chandler.

Braybrooke, D., & Lindblom, C. E. (1963). *A strategy of decision.* New York, NY: Free Press.

Eisner, E. W. (1991). *The enlightened eye: Qualitative inquiry and the enhancement of educational practice.* New York, NY: Macmillan.

Mezirow, J. (1990). How critical reflection triggers transformative learning. In J. Mezirow & Associates (Ed.), *Fostering critical reflection in adulthood: A guide to transformative and emancipatory learning.* San Francisco, CA: Jossey-Bass.

Patton, M. Q. (1997). *Utilization-focused evaluation: The new century text.* Thousand Oaks, CA: Sage.

Senge, P. M. (2000). The academy as learning community: Contradiction in terms or realizable future? In A. F. Lucas & Associates (Eds.), *Leading academic change: Essential roles for department chairs* (pp. 275-300). San Francisco, CA: Jossey-Bass.

Shulman, L. S. (1995, January). Teaching as community property. Address to AAHE Forum on Faculty Roles and Rewards. San Diego, CA.

Smith, V. B. (1998). *The futures project: A two-year activity of 18 independent colleges and universities in California.* Final report to James Irvine Foundation.

Tierney, W. G. (1999). *Building the responsive campus: Creating high performance colleges and universities.* Thousand Oaks, CA: Sage.

Zemsky, R., & Massy, W. F. (1993, May/June). On reversing the ratchet: Restructuring in colleges and universities. *Change, 25,* 56-62.

8

ENHANCING DEPARTMENTAL QUALITY

Thinking without actions is futile; but action

without thinking is fatal.

—James Colvard

It's what you learn after you know it all that counts.

—Earl Weaver

INTRODUCTION

In this last chapter, I want to revisit the question I posed at the beginning of this volume—What characterizes a quality department or program?—and address two others as a way of summarizing its central themes: What are the keys to creating departments that work? And What can department faculty and their chairs do to bring about these cultures of excellence?

CHARACTERISTICS OF THE QUALITY DEPARTMENT

Recall the two lists of characteristics of quality departments in Chapter 1: These were generated by two groups of mostly department chairs who were asked to come up with descriptors of quality departments at their own institutions. A synthesis of these two lists follows:

Characteristics of Quality Departments: Faculty and Administrators

- Shared mission and vision
- Balance in focus on students, community, institution, faculty
- Best possible students consistent with institutional mission
- Commitment to excellence in teaching and student learning
- A high value on professional autonomy
- Significant student engagement with faculty and each other
- Active scholarship by students and faculty
- Collaboration and self-reflection
- Innovation; flexibility to change
- Collegiality and a strong sense of academic community
- Respect for diversity of opinion; creative tension
- Continuous evaluation of programs and use of assessment data
- Strong ties with alumni and industry
- Visionary leadership from faculty and chair

MARKERS OF QUALITY IN ACADEMIC DEPARTMENTS

I'd now like to add three other sources of wisdom on markers of quality in academic departments.

First Source

The first is from Walvoord and her colleagues (2000) who undertook an extensive review of the literature on departmental effectiveness, and derived this list of traits of healthy departments:

> **Self-knowledge:** understanding their own and other cultures, environments, assumptions, values, and mental models

Systems thinking: exploring and understanding how all elements of an organization and its environment interact

Open, productive interaction: valuing greater closeness, more time together, more synergistic interaction, and healthy ways of managing conflict

High freedom for individuals: emphasizing high freedom for individuals and valuing personal mastery

Outward focus on environment, stakeholders, and results: evaluating the effects of the group's decisions so that group learning can take place

Entrepreneurialism: valuing entrepreneurial and imaginative solutions born from interaction and commitment of the members of the group

Fostering individuals' commitment to the well-being of the group

An emphasis on group and individual learning: changing behaviors on the basis of examination of the department's values and outcomes of its work

Gathering and acting on information about the department's culture and environment

Good leaders: supporting leaders who are open, collaborative, and strive for joint decisions, but also are proactive in guiding the department (pp. 6-7)

Note the themes of engagement, critical reflection, and honest collegiality, all points of emphasis in this book. Note also the overlaps with the chairs' list—none of whom had read Walvoord's book!

Second Source

The second source is William Massy's seven core quality principles (2001), based on his extensive experience as higher education researcher and quality guru. Despite his use of total quality management lingo here and there, the similarities of his principles to those just presented are also striking:

- Define education quality in terms of outcomes.
- Focus on the process of teaching and learning.
- Strive for coherence in curriculum and process.
- Work collaboratively to achieve mutual involvement and support.
- Base decisions on facts whenever possible.
- Minimize controllable quality variation.
- Make continuous quality improvement a top priority. (p. 50)

Third Source

The third source I've already cited extensively: Haworth and Conrad's (1997) engagement theory of program quality, based upon interviews with 781 people in 47 graduate (master's) programs. Their theory is reprinted as Figure 8.1.

According to Haworth and Conrad, high quality programs are those which "provide enriching learning experiences that positively affect students' growth and development" (1997, p. 27). This occurs when departments invest significant time and energy to create and sustain five clusters of attributes:

Diverse and engaged participants: by recruiting and supporting faculty and students having diverse perspectives and providing a setting for constructive discourse

Participatory cultures: marked by shared purposes, a supportive community, and freedom to take reasonable risks

Interactive teaching and learning: through active and hands-on engagement with the subject matter

Connected program requirements: leading to more unified understandings and tangible learning products

Adequate resources for students and faculty: in the

form of requisite supplies, equipment, facilities, and library
and computing resources

FIGURE 8.1
ENGAGEMENT THEORY OF PROGRAM QUALITY

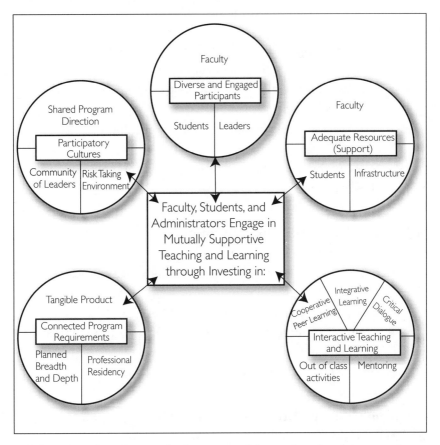

While Haworth and Conrad's theory was delimited to developing and sustaining high-quality educational programs, particularly graduate programs,
their framework is useful for describing characteristics of quality programs
as a whole as well. Notice, again, the substantial overlap with the previous
lists, especially their clusters 1 and 2. Haworth and Conrad suggest that
their engagement thesis makes diverse and engaged participants and participatory cultures first among equals as markers of departmental quality.
Judging from the overlap, many chairs and faculty would agree.

CHARACTERISTICS OF A QUALITY ACADEMIC DEPARTMENT: A SYNTHESIS

Pulling these four diverse sources together—based, respectively, on practical experience, research, management theory, and grounded theory—suggests the following synthesis:

A Diverse and Supportive Academic Community

- A high value on professional autonomy
- Faculty and students from diverse backgrounds and with diverse perspectives
- A setting for constructive discourse: respect for diversity of opinion; creative tension
- Support for innovation, entrepreneurialism, and reasonable risk
- Flexibility to change

A Culture of Collective Responsibility

- Shared mission and vision
- Balance in focus on students, community, institution, discipline
- Individuals' commitment to the well-being of the group
- Group commitment to the welfare of the institution and the community
- Significant student engagement with faculty and each other

A Commitment to Excellence in Teaching, Student Learning, and Scholarship

- Best possible students consistent with institutional mission
- Active and hands-on engagement of students with the subject matter
- Connected program requirements and coherent curricula
- Active scholarship by students and faculty

A Culture of Critical Reflection

- An emphasis on individual and collective self-reflection

- Continuous evaluation of programs and careful use of assessment data
- An emphasis on both group and individual learning

Visionary Leadership from Faculty and Chair
- Openness, collaboration, and joint decision-making
- Systems thinking
- Visionary thinking

Adequate Resources for Students and Faculty
- Requisite supplies, equipment, facilities
- Library and computing resources

Keep in mind that stakeholders other than faculty and administration will have other lists. My guess, however, based upon numerous conversations with these other groups, is that the quality lists will overlap considerably. Students and parents will be relatively more concerned about the instrumental value of the program (that is, how well it prepares students for their chosen careers), while boards and trustees will be relatively more concerned about economics and productivity indicators such as enrollment and credit-hour generation. But an academic department reflecting most or all of the qualities above is likely to find favor beyond its own faculty and the central administration of the institution.

CREATING THE QUALITY DEPARTMENT

Creating a culture of quality is not a solo enterprise. It requires joint effort, an amalgam of the talents and perspectives of the chair and the faculty.

Department Chairs as Agents for Quality Work

Departments don't lead themselves. They have chairs for a reason. And their leaders are also called "chairs" for a reason. They're not bosses or foremen, nor are they simply colleagues with larger offices and 12-month contracts. They are leaders, but leaders of a special sort known only to the academy. They manage the administrative details of the department, of course, but they are also responsible for defining and shaping the work of the department, balancing individual faculty interests with the collective interests of the whole. This, more than anything, is what sets department chairs in colleges and universities apart from middle managers in other organizations. They are facilitators, negotiators, meaning makers, and bridge builders. Here's what the Pew Higher Education Roundtable observed about the special role of department chairs: "More than any other figure in the department, it is the chair who must convene faculty conversations that, precisely because they raise tough questions, evoke meaningful answers defining the nature of their community's work" (1996, p. 10). Many good books have been written expressly for the purpose of helping develop the leadership skills of department chairs: Gmelch and Miskin (1993); Tucker (1993); Lucas (1994); Seagren, Cresswell, and Wheeler (1995); Leaming (1998); Hecht, Higgerson, Gmelch, and Tucker (1999); Bensimon, Ward, and Sanders (2000); and Lucas and Associates (2000). I won't recapitulate their good advice. I do, however, want to make a few points which convey the department chair's responsibilities for enhancing departmental quality.

It's hard to imagine having a quality department without a quality chair. Quality chairs do the following things:

They understand the unique dynamics of an academic culture. They don't fall prey to seeing their department as simply a collection of faculty with similar academic interests; but neither do they succumb to the notion of the department as a team, at least not in the traditional sense of the term. They realize that faculty are team members only in a limited sense, and will resist being characterized as such. With apologies to my colleague, Ann Lucas, who has written extensively about departments as teams (1994, 2000), I don't believe that "team" fairly characterizes what academic departments are about, at least not fully. A "team," according to Katzenbach and Smith (1993), is "a small number of people with complementary skills who are committed to a common purpose, set of performance goals, and approach for which they hold themselves mutually accountable" (p. 112).

There's a lot to like in this definition as applied to academic departments: the notion of complementarity and respect for difference, a common purpose (departmental mission), and acceptance of collective responsibility. What the definition leaves out, however, are attributes that are critical to a quality academic culture: a reliance on autonomy and creativity of individual faculty rather than team products; the room for, even need for, constructive contention; and, especially in large departments, the recognition that departments have multiple missions and thus usually do not have clear tasks that all members share.

To my mind, a better way of thinking about departments is as communities of interest: organizational units where members share common academic interests and purposes, recognize and value diverse roles, and take collective responsibility for the work they do, without neglecting their individual autonomy and commitment to academic freedom. Viewing departments as communities of interest also signals the importance of political processes as key determinants of quality. If departmental quality is viewed as the successful negotiation of multiple interests, then it follows that faculty have a communal interest, or stake, in that negotiation.

They concentrate on creating settings for quality work and focus on identifying and removing barriers to quality work. I noted in Chapter 2 that available research on faculty motivation suggests that while reward systems must be in sync with desired behavior, chairs and other academic leaders must affirm the importance of intrinsic motivation as the central source of energy for quality work. The problem therefore is not how to motivate faculty—something most chairs feel inadequate to do anyway—but rather how to nurture a work environment characterized by high autonomy, significant opportunities for recognition, a strong academic community, and a high potential for personal efficacy.

They understand that creating and sustaining a shared vision is a vitally important function, as long as the vision is ambitious, malleable, and flexible with respect to differences in interpretation. Successful chairs don't waste their departments' time with empty exercises in crafting mission and vision statements. They do, however,

understand how important it is to develop these shared purposes inductively: to frame departmental mission by abstracting from the work individual faculty do, negotiated with institutional priorities; and to frame a
shared vision by abstracting from the values and aspirations individual
faculty have. They understand also that the best visions are bold and
even audacious, while always negotiable on the basis of new information
and emerging opportunities. They don't let themselves be held hostage
to the myopia and linear thinking of formal strategic plans, but rather
give themselves and their departments the freedom to engage in experimentation, innovation, and reasonable risk-taking within the context of
their shared vision.

They introduce "difficult conversations" (Lucas, 2000) *about
matters of importance to the department.* They aren't afraid to
address issues directly and put them on the table. They recognize the
emptiness of "hollowed collegiality" (Massy, Wilger, & Colbeck, 1994)
and the inertia it creates, and realize that transformative growth and
change occurs most frequently through discomfort. They also recognize
the point at which constructive contention becomes academic games-
manship, in the form of endless analysis and criticism.

*They are good listeners and remain respectful of the collec-
tive wisdom of their colleagues.* Faculty members are semi-
autonomous players in semi-autonomous units. In academic cultures,
multiple perspectives are not only to be tolerated but also respected. At
the same time, successful chairs recognize potential points of consensus
and are able to capture and articulate them.

*They frame issues clearly, delineate options, and lay out con-
sequences of options chosen.* Quality chairs know that true consensus
is not always possible or even desirable. They understand that their role
requires them to make tough, even painful, decisions for the good of
the whole. They also realize, however, that difficult decisions will be
both more informed and more bearable when they invite, even co-opt,
the faculty into the process.

*They create ways for the department to reflect critically
about its work as a unit.* Without that, the faculty may be satisfied

and productive as individual teachers and scholars, but the department as a whole will be unfocused, its work will not cohere, and the interests of its stakeholders (especially students) will likely suffer. Quality chairs take a proactive and inside-out approach to quality assessment, not waiting for academic administrators or political forces outside the institution to dictate the terms. Instead, they work with the department to identify key questions the department as a whole needs to address, sources of evidence that will inform these questions most usefully, and ways of making meaning and taking appropriate action.

Faculty as Agents for Quality Work

In Chapter 3, I noted how faculty resistance is one of the usual suspects deemed responsible for the sorry state of many institutional change initiatives. For better or worse, the reputation is not entirely undeserved. Obstructing change is not always a bad thing, as the fate of such misguided initiatives as zero-based budgeting and management by objectives has so clearly demonstrated. Still, as hard as it is to imagine a quality department without a quality chair, it's even harder to imagine a quality department without faculty who are committed to quality work; and as I argued in Chapter 4, quality work by a department is more than just the sum of quality work by individuals. The department as a whole must commit to critical reflection, growth, and change as a unit. Faculty in departments like these mirror the behavior of quality chairs. They also do the following:

They, like their chairs, understand the unique dynamics of an academic culture. They understand the necessity of balancing individual with collective agendas, individual entrepreneurship with departmental priorities. They feel individually and collectively responsible for the department's success: They commit their energies to common goals even if these are related only indirectly to their individual work. They resist the temptation to claim proprietary rights to their courses and other work belonging most appropriately to the department.

They know themselves well and have a clear sense of niche within their departments. They are honest with themselves about who they are, what motivates them, and what they have to contribute to the common good.

They transcend comfortable collaboration (Walvoord et al., 2000) by participating freely and openly in issues of importance to the department. They recognize the dangers of hollowed collegiality and understand that attending to issues that matter is in their long-term interest. They respect each other enough to go beyond mere tolerance of difference, and so they give and accept constructive criticism willingly. They share their work publicly, including their teaching, as part of the work of the department.

They dream, they aspire, and they understand how their personal visions translate into shared visions.

They acknowledge how the needs of their faculty colleagues change as they pass through their career trajectories: They encourage junior faculty by mentoring and socializing them and learning from the fresh perspectives they bring, and they encourage senior faculty by calling upon their experience and institutional history.

They participate fully in departmental governance. They don't treat academic administration as a necessary evil or as the destination of colleagues who are unfit to do the real work of the academy. They understand academic decision-making as a process in which they all have a stake. They avoid the temptation to demand full consultation on all decisions while avoiding responsibility for implementing these decisions. They make it their business to understand budget processes, resource allocation procedures, and alternative uses of funds. And finally, they understand that their interests will not always be congruent with those of the department or the institution.

They apply the qualities of critical inquiry—qualities they have learned so well as applied to their disciplinary scholarship—to their own work. They have learned that quality work requires them to devote some of their time to reflecting carefully, based both on assessment data and their own experience, on what they are doing, why they are doing it, and whether the effects of what they do are in the best interests of their chief beneficiaries, namely their students.

The quality of an institution is marked, more than anything else, by the quality of its departments and its academic programs. Departments aren't mere organizational units charged with carrying out the purpose of the institution; rather, they are semi-autonomous organizations themselves, and their vitality is what makes institutions tick. Without program quality, what happens in the rest of the institution makes little difference. And thus I think it's a huge mistake to write departments off, as some have, as hopeless anachronisms, forever standing in the way of needed change. I subscribe instead to the view held by Walvoord and her colleagues, (2000), who said this:

> *Departments are not merely silos or barriers or dinosaurs; they are adapting organisms trying to accomplish difficult and complex tasks in difficult and complex circumstances. It is not clear whether departments can change sufficiently to be effective in the rapidly changing world they face. But the only hope for change lies in building upon departments' own structures, cultures, and avenues of potential change. (p. 2)*

In other words, quality happens from the inside out. Through honest engagement, and critical self-inquiry, academic departments can change the message of the skeptics.

REFERENCES

Bensimon, E. M., Ward, K., & Sanders, K. (2000). *The department chair's role in developing new faculty into teachers and scholars.* Bolton, MA: Anker.

Gmelch, W. H., & Miskin, V. D. (1993). *Leadership skills for department chairs.* Bolton, MA: Anker.

Haworth, J. G., & Conrad, C. F. (1997). *Emblems of quality in higher education: Developing and sustaining high-quality programs.* Needham Heights, MA: Allyn & Bacon.

Hecht, I., Higgerson, M. L., Gmelch, W. H., & Tucker, A. (1999). *The department chair as academic leader.* Phoenix, AZ: Oryx.

Katzenbach, J. R., & Smith, D. K. (1993, March/April). The discipline of teams. *Harvard Business Review,* 111-120.

Knight Higher Education Collaborative. (1996, February). Double agent. *Policy Perspectives, 6* (3).

Leaming, D. R. (1998). *Academic leadership: A practical guide to chairing the department.* Bolton, MA: Anker.

Lucas, A. F. (1994). *Strengthening departmental leadership: A team-building guide for chairs in colleges and universities.* San Francisco, CA: Jossey-Bass.

Lucas, A. F., & Associates. (2000). *Leading academic change: Essential roles for department chairs.* San Francisco, CA: Jossey-Bass.

Massy, W. F. (2001, July/August). Making quality work. *University Business, 4,* 44-50.

Massy, W. F., Wilger, A. K., & Colbeck, C. (1994, July/August). Overcoming "hollowed" collegiality. *Change, 26* (4), 10-20.

Seagren, A. T., Creswell, J. W., & Wheeler, D. W. (1995). *The department chair: New roles, responsibilities, and challenges.* ASHE-ERIC Higher Education Report, No. 1. Washington, DC: George Washington University, Graduate School of Education and Human Development. (ED 363 164)

Tucker, A. (1993). *Chairing the academic department* (3rd ed.). Washington, DC: American Council on Education/Oryx.

Walvoord, B. E., Carey, A. K., Smith, H. L., Soled, S. W., Way, P. K., & Zorn, D. (2000). *Academic departments: How they work, how they change.* ASHE-ERIC Higher Education Report, 27 (8). San Francisco, CA: Jossey-Bass.

appendix

DEPARTMENTS THAT WORK:

WHAT THEY DO

In this appendix, I've distilled and pulled together some of the key characteristics of departments that work.

CHAPTER 1: THE CONCEPT OF ACADEMIC QUALITY

Departments that work:

- Recognize that quality can never be assumed just because "we in the academy know best."
- Understand the power of peer review as the only form of public accountability over which the academy and its faculty have any direct control.
- Realize that true academic quality is not synonymous with marketability, productivity, efficiency, or even effectiveness, but rather is a complex and multidimensional concept which is defined by how the department engages with its constituencies.

CHAPTER 2: MOTIVATION FOR QUALITY WORK

Departments that work:

- Recognize the importance—but also the limitations—of external motivators such as salary, promotion, and tenure as forces for quality work.
- Understand the power of internal motivation, especially the following:
  - Autonomy
  - Community
  - Recognition
  - Efficacy
- Employ strategies which most enhance faculty motivation:
  - Align mission, roles, and rewards
  - Engage faculty meaningfully
  - Identify and take advantage of disorienting dilemmas
  - Help faculty develop niches
  - Encourage faculty experimentation, assessment, and reflection

- Focus on organizational motivation by finding ways for faculty to identify with the department and the institution
- Know that they are making a difference

CHAPTER 3: EVALUATING QUALITY IN ACADEMIC PROGRAMS

Departments that work:
- Have thrown off a compliance mentality regarding quality assurance, and instead have embraced academic quality as something for which they are all mutually responsible.
- Acknowledge the following organizational conditions and strive to enhance them:
  - A leadership of engagement
  - A culture of evidence
  - A culture of peer collaboration and peer review
  - A respect for difference
  - Evaluation with consequence
- Use flexible evaluation policies and encourage central administration to do likewise.
- Treat evaluation criteria and evidence with skepticism and understand the importance of reasoned professional judgment.

CHAPTER 4: CREATING THE ENGAGED DEPARTMENT

Departments that work:
- Recognize the dangers of a faculty culture dominated by specialization, isolation, and privatization.
- Recognize, in contrast, the power of the faculty as a collective, characterized by:
  - Work that is contextual to the institution's mission and central character
  - Mutual accountability, especially as regards the curriculum
  - A balance between professional autonomy and social responsibility

- ◆ Greater political clout within the institution
- Behave in ways consistent with the following principles:
  - ◆ The work of the institution, defined in terms of its social compact and the collective work of its departmental units, frames the choices for departmental work.
  - ◆ The department is guided both by the aggregate work of its member faculty, and by how it adds value as a whole to the institution.
  - ◆ The work of the department provides a basis for framing the work individual faculty members do.
  - ◆ Faculty members are guided in their choices both by how they add value to their disciplines and how they add value to the work of their departments.
  - ◆ Choices, whether made by individual faculty members or by departments as a whole, are the product of negotiation with key stakeholders.

CHAPTER 5: NEGOTIATING DEPARTMENTAL VALUES

Departments that work:

- Understand that departmental quality is in the eye of the beholder, and thus that quality is contingent upon the negotiation of multiple interests.
- Periodically renegotiate quality standards, in particular, they:
  - ◆ Identify the department's stakeholders
  - ◆ Engage in responsive focusing, starting with departmental faculty and working outward from those with most to those with least at stake
  - ◆ Pull together the claims, concerns, and issues from the stakeholder groups and sort them by strength of interest
  - ◆ Compare faculty standards with those of other stakeholders, starting again with those most central to the department

♦ Choose a negotiating position which advances the department's interest at the least political cost, and negotiate quality standards accordingly

CHAPTER 6: FINDING EVIDENCE OF QUALITY AND QUALITY EVIDENCE

Departments that work:

- Ask the right questions, namely questions which:
  - ♦ Are empirical
  - ♦ Have more than one possible answer
  - ♦ The department and others truly care about
  - ♦ When answered will lead to productive action
- Know how to convert data to evidence.
- Look for congruence between potential evidence and the department's values and goals.
- Show the link between evidence and questions to which the evidence is addressed.
- Understand the limits of any data collection tool.
- Compile evidence using multiple sources of data.
- Assess the comprehensiveness of evidence as a set, relative to the information needed.
- Are able to answer "what if" questions, such as, What will we do if the evidence shows...?

CHAPTER 7: MAKING MEANING OF QUALITY EVIDENCE

Departments that work:

- Recognize that nothing is simple, yet search for simple representations of data without engaging in reductionistic thinking.
- Connect reflection with action by:
  - ♦ Taking stock of what the evidence suggests
  - ♦ Revisiting claims and concerns in light of the evidence
  - ♦ Considering how the evidence addresses key claims and concerns of the department's constituencies

     ✦ Using discussion to fashion a plan of action, one that is
founded on strategic thinking but also recognizes the
value of experimentation and risk taking
- Recognize that the best kind of action is that which leads
to further reflection and organizational learning.

CHAPTER 8: ENHANCING DEPARTMENTAL QUALITY

Departments that work have these qualities in common:
- A diverse and supportive academic community.
- A culture of collective responsibility.
- A commitment to excellence in teaching, student learning,
and scholarship.
- A culture of critical reflection.
- Visionary leadership from faculty and the chair.
- Adequate resources for students and faculty.

Departments that work have chairs who:
- Understand the unique dynamics of an academic culture.
- Concentrate on creating settings for quality work and
focus on identifying and removing barriers to quality work.
- Understand that creating and sustaining a shared vision is
a vitally important function, as long as the vision is ambitious, malleable, and flexible with respect to differences in
interpretation.
- Introduce difficult conversations about matters of importance to the department.
- Are good listeners and remain respectful of the collective
wisdom of their colleagues.
- Frame issues clearly, delineate options, and lay out likely
consequences of options chosen.
- Create ways for the department to reflect critically about
its work as a unit.

Departments that work have faculty who:
- Understand, like their chairs, the unique dynamics of an
academic culture.

- Know themselves well and have a clear sense of niche within their departments.
- Transcend comfortable collaboration by participating freely and openly in issues of importance to the department.
- Dream, aspire, and understand how their personal visions translate into shared visions.
- Acknowledge how the needs of their faculty colleagues change as they pass through their career trajectories.
- Participate freely in departmental governance.
- Apply qualities of critical inquiry to their own work.

bibliography

REFERENCES

Alpert, D. (1986). Performance and paralysis: The organizational context of the American research university. *Journal of Higher Education, 56* (3), 76-102.

Association of American Colleges and Universities. (1985). *Integrity in the college curriculum: A report to the academic community.* Washington, DC: Author.

American Association of University Professors. (1940, 1995). *AAUP policy documents and reports.* Washington, DC: author.

Association of American Colleges. (1985). *Integrity in the college curriculum: A report to the academic community.* Washington, DC: Author.

Austin, A. E., & Baldwin, R. G. (1992). *Faculty collaboration: Enhancing the quality of scholarship and teaching.* Washington, DC: ASHE/ERIC Higher Education Report.

Baldridge, J. V. (1971). *Power and conflict in the university: Research in the sociology of complex organizations.* New York, NY: Wiley.

Baldwin, R. G., & Krotseng, M. V. (1985). *Incentives in the academy: Issues and options.* New Directions for Higher Education, No. 51. San Francisco, CA: Jossey-Bass.

Bandura, A. (1977). *Social learning theory.* Englewood Cliffs, NJ: Prentice-Hall.

Bee, H. L. (2000). *The journey of adulthood* (4th ed.). Upper Saddle River, NJ: Prentice-Hall.

Bennett, J. B. (1998). *Collegial professionalism : The academy, individualism, and the common good.* Phoenix, AZ: Oryx.

Bensimon, E. M., & O'Neill, H. F., Jr. (1998). Collaborative effort to measure faculty work. *Liberal Education, 84* (4).

Bensimon, E. M., Ward, K., & Sanders, K. (2000). *The department chair's role in developing new faculty into teachers and scholars.* Bolton, MA: Anker.

Blau, P. M., & Scott, W. R. (1962). *Formal organizations: A comparative approach.* San Francisco, CA: Chandler.

Boyer, E. (1990). *Scholarship reconsidered: Priorities of the professoriate.* Princeton, NJ: Carnegie Foundation for the Advancement of Teaching.

Braskamp, L. A. (1997). *On being responsive and responsible.* CHEA Chronicle No. 6. Washington, DC: Council for Higher Education Accreditation.

Braybrooke, D., & Lindblom, C. E. (1963). *A strategy of decision.* New York, NY: Free Press.

Brookfield, S. D. (1995). *Becoming a critically reflective teacher.* San Francisco, CA: Jossey-Bass.

Burke, J. C. (1999, July/August). The assessment anomaly: If everyone's doing it why isn't more getting done? *Assessment Update, 11,* 4.

Cervero, R. M., & Wilson, A. L. (1994). *Planning responsibly for adult education: A guide to negotiating power and interests.* San Francisco, CA: Jossey-Bass.

Clark, B. R. (1987). *The academic life: Small worlds, different worlds.* Princeton, NJ: Carnegie Foundation for the Advancement of Teaching.

Csikszentmihalyi, M. (1990). *Flow: The psychology of optimal experience.* New York, NY: Harper-Collins.

Dewey, J. (1933). *How we think: A restatement of the relation of reflective thinking to the educative process.* Lexington, MA: D. C. Heath.

Diamond, R. M. (1993). Changing priorities and the faculty reward system. In R. M. Diamond & B. E. Adam (Eds.), *Recognizing faculty work: Reward systems for the year 2000.* New Directions for Higher Education, No. 81. San Francisco, CA: Jossey-Bass.

Dill, D. D. (1999). *Implementing academic audits: Lessons learned in Europe and Asia.* Unpublished manuscript. Chapel Hill, NC: University of North Carolina.

Dill, D. D., Massy, W. F., Williams, P. R., & Cook, C. M. (1996, September/October). Accreditation and academic quality assurance: Can we get there from here? *Change, 28* (5),17-24.

Eisner, E. W. (1991). *The enlightened eye: Qualitative inquiry and the enhancement of educational practice.* New York, NY: Macmillan.

Ewell, P. (2002). *Evidence guide: A guide to using evidence in the accreditation process.* Alameda, CA: Western Association of Schools and Colleges.

Fairweather, J. (1996). *Faculty work and the public trust: Restoring the value of teaching and public service in American academic life.* Boston, MA: Allyn & Bacon.

Ferren, A. S., & Slavings, R. (2000). *Investing in quality: Tools for improving curricular efficiency.* Washington, DC: Association of American Colleges and Universities.

Froh, R. C., Menges, R. J., & Walker, C. J. (1993). Revitalizing faculty work through intrinsic rewards. In R. M. Diamond & B. E. Adam (Eds.), *Recognizing faculty work: Reward systems for the year 2000* (pp. 87-95). New Directions for Higher Education, No. 81. San Francisco, CA: Jossey-Bass.

Gaff, J. G., Pruitt-Logan, A. S., Weibl, R. A., & Associates. (2000). *Building the faculty we need: Colleges and universities working together.* Washington, DC: Association of American Colleges and Universities.

Garvin, D. A. (1988). *Managing quality: The strategic and competitive edge.* New York: NY: Free Press.

Gelmon, S. B. (1997). *Intentional improvement: The deliberate linkage of assessment and accreditation.* Presentation to the 1997 AAHE

Conference on Assessment and Quality. Washington, DC: American Association for Higher Education.

Gmelch, W. H. (1995). Department chairs under siege: Resolving the web of conflict. In S. Holton (Ed.), *Conflict management in higher education*. New Directions for Higher Education, No. 92. San Francisco, CA: Jossey-Bass.

Guba, E. G., & Lincoln, Y. S. (1989). *Fourth generation evaluation.* Newbury Park, CA: Sage.

Haworth, J. G., & Conrad, C. F. (1997). *Emblems of quality in higher education: Developing and sustaining high-quality programs.* Needham Heights, MA: Allyn & Bacon.

Hecht, I., Higgerson, M. L., Gmelch, W. H., & Tucker, A. (1999). *The department chair as academic leader.* Phoenix, AZ: Oryx.

Holton, S. (Ed.). (1998). *Mending the cracks in the ivory tower: Strategies for conflict management in higher education.* Bolton, MA: Anker.

Joint Committee on Standards for Educational Evaluation, James R. Sanders, chair. (1994). *The program evaluation standards: How to assess evaluations of educational programs.* Thousand Oaks, CA: Sage.

Katzenbach, J. R., & Smith, D. K. (1993, March/April). The discipline of teams. *Harvard Business Review,* 111-120.

Kerr, S. (1975). On the folly of rewarding A, while hoping for B. *Academy of Management Journal, 18,* 769-783.

Knight Higher Education Collaborative. (1991, September). An end to sanctuary. *Policy Perspectives, 3* (4).

Knight Higher Eductation Collaborative. (1996, February). Double agent. *Policy Perspectives, 6* (3).

Knight Higher Education Collaborative. (2000, March). The data made me do it. *Policy Perspectives, 9* (2).

Kohn, A. (1993). *Punished by rewards: The trouble with gold stars, incentive plans, A's, praise, and other bribes.* Boston, MA: Houghton Mifflin.

Langenburg, D. N. (1992, September 2). Team scholarship could help strengthen scholarly traditions. *The Chronicle of Higher Education,* p. A64.

Lucas, A. F. (1994). *Strengthening departmental leadership: A team-building guide for chairs in colleges and universities.* San Francisco, CA: Jossey-Bass.

Lucas, A. F., & Associates. (2000). *Leading academic change: Essential roles for department chairs.* San Francisco, CA: Jossey-Bass.

Massy, W. F. (2001, July/August). Making quality work. *University Business, 4,* 44-50.

Massy, W. F., Wilger, A. K., & Colbeck, C. (1994, July/August). Overcoming "hollowed" collegiality. *Change, 26* (4), 10-20.

McKeachie, W. J. (1993). *What we know about faculty motivation.* Presentation to first AAHE Forum on Faculty Roles and Rewards, San Antonio, TX (audiotape).

McMillan, J. H., Wergin, J. F., Forsyth, D. R., & Brown, J. C. (1986). Student ratings of instruction: A summary of literature. *Instructional Evaluation, 9* (1), 2-9.

McMillin, L. A., & Berberet, J. (Eds.). (2002). *A new academic compact: Revisioning the relationship between faculty and their institutions.* Bolton, MA: Anker.

Menges R., & Associates. (1999). *Faculty in new jobs: A guide to settling in, becoming established, and building institutional support.* San Francisco, CA: Jossey-Bass.

Messick, S. (1994). *Validity of psychological assessment: Validation of inferences from persons' responses and performances as scientific inquiry into score meaning.* Research Report RR-94-45. ERIC Identifier: ED380496

Mezirow, J. (1990). How critical reflection triggers transformative learning. In J. Mezirow & Associates (Eds.), *Fostering critical reflection in adulthood: A guide to transformative and emancipatory learning.* San Francisco, CA: Jossey-Bass.

National Center for Postsecondary Improvement. (1999, September/October). Revolution or evolution? Gauging the impact of institutional student-assessment strategies. *Change,* 53-56.

National Center for Postsecondary Improvement. (2000, March/April). Why is research the rule? The impact of incentive systems on faculty behavior. *Change,* 53-56.

National Research Council. (2000). *How people learn: Brain, mind, experience, and school* (expanded edition). Washington, DC: National Academy Press.

Palmer, P. J. (1998). *The courage to teach: Exploring the inner landscape of a teacher's life.* San Francisco, CA: Jossey-Bass.

Palomba, C. A., & Banta, T. W. (1999). *Assessment essentials: Planning, implementing, and improving assessment in higher education.* San Francisco, CA: Jossey-Bass.

Patton, M. Q. (1990). *Qualitative evaluation and research methods.* Newbury Park, CA: Sage.

Patton, M. Q. (1997). *Utilization-focused evaluation: The new century text.* Thousand Oaks, CA: Sage.

Peterson, M. W., & Einarson, M. K. (2001). What are colleges doing about student assessment? Does it make a difference? *Journal of Higher Education, 72,* 629-669.

Pirsig, R. M. (1974). *Zen and the art of motorcycle maintenance: An inquiry into values.* New York, NY: Bantam.

Polyani, M. (1967). *The tacit dimension.* New York, NY: Doubleday.

Preskill, H., & Torres, R. T. (1998). *Evaluative inquiry for learning in organizations.* Thousand Oaks, CA: Sage.

Pruett, E. S. (2001). *Restructuring faculty workload: A qualitative study of the effects of faculty role differentiation on senior faculty members' perception of the quality of their work lives.* Doctoral dissertation, Virginia Commonwealth University.

Rice, R. E. (1996). *Making a place for the new American scholar. New pathways: Faculty career and employment for the 21st Century.* Working Paper Series, Inquiry No. 1. Washington, DC: AAHE.

Schuster, J. H., Wheeler, D. W., & Associates. (1990). *Enhancing faculty careers: Strategies for development and renewal.* San Francisco, CA: Jossey-Bass.

Seagren, A. T., Creswell, J. W., & Wheeler, D. W. (1995). *The department chair: New roles, responsibilities, and challenges.* ASHE-ERIC Higher Education Report, No. 1. Washington, DC: George Washington University, Graduate School of Education and Human Development. (ED 363 164)

Senge, P. M. (2000). The academy as learning community: Contradiction in terms or realizable future? In A. F. Lucas & Associates (Eds.), *Leading academic change: Essential roles for department chairs* (pp. 275-300). San Francisco, CA: Jossey-Bass.

Seymour, D. T. (1993). *On Q: Causing quality in higher education.* Phoenix, AZ: Oryx.

Shulman, L. S. (1993). Teaching as community property: Putting and end to pedagogical solitude. *Change, 25* (6), 6-7.

Shulman, L. S. (1995, January). *Teaching as community property.* Address to AAHE Forum on Faculty Roles and Rewards. San Diego, CA.

Smith, V. B. (1998). *The futures project: A two-year activity of 18 independent colleges and universities in California.* Final report to James Irvine Foundation.

Staw, B. M. (1983). Motivation research versus the art of faculty management. In J. L. Bess (Ed.), *College and university organization:*

Insights from the behavioral sciences. New York: NYU Press.

Tierney, W. G. (1999). *Building the responsive campus: Creating high performance colleges and universities.* Thousand Oaks, CA: Sage.

Tompkins, J. P. (1992, November/December). The way we live now. *Change, 24,* 12-19.

Trower, C., Austin, A., & Sorcinelli, M. (2001, May). Paradise lost: How the academy converts enthusiastic recruits into early-career doubters. *AAHE Bulletin, 53* (9), 3-6.

Tucker, A. (1993). *Chairing the academic department* (3rd ed.). Washington, DC: American Council on Education/Oryx.

United States Office of Scientific Research and Development. (1945). *Science, the endless frontier: A report to the President by Vannevar Bush.* Washington, DC: Author.

University of California at Los Angeles Higher Education Research Institute. (1997). *The American college teacher: National norms for the 1995-96 HERI faculty survey.* Los Angeles, CA: Author.

Walvoord, B. E., Carey, A. K., Smith, H. L., Soled, S. W., Way, P. K., & Zorn, D. (2000). *Academic departments: How they work, how they change.* ASHE-ERIC Higher Education Report, 27 (8). San Francisco, CA: Jossey-Bass.

Wergin, J. F. (1976). Evaluation of organizational policymaking: A political model. *Review of Educational Research, 46* (1), 75-115.

Wergin, J. F. (1994). *The collaborative department: How five campuses are inching toward cultures of collective responsibility.* Washington, DC: AAHE.

Wergin, J. F. (1998). Assessment of programs and units. Presentation at the 1998 AAHE Assessment Conference. Reprinted in *Architecture for change: Information as foundation.* Washington, DC: AAHE.

Wergin, J. F., & Swingen, J. N. (2000). *Departmental assessment: How some colleges are effectively evaluating the collective work of faculty.* Washington, DC: AAHE.

Zemsky, R., & Massy, W. F. (1993, May/June). On reversing the ratchet: Restructuring in colleges and universities. *Change, 25,* 56-62.

index